50 Holiday Cookie Recipes for Home

By: Kelly Johnson

Table of Contents

- Classic Sugar Cookies
- Gingerbread Cookies
- Peppermint Chocolate Crinkle Cookies
- Snickerdoodles
- Linzer Cookies
- Thumbprint Cookies (with assorted jams)
- White Chocolate Macadamia Nut Cookies
- Chocolate-Dipped Shortbread Cookies
- Cranberry Orange Biscotti
- Red Velvet Crinkle Cookies
- Almond Butter Cookies
- Lemon Glazed Cookies
- Eggnog Cookies
- Pistachio Cranberry Biscotti
- Chocolate Peppermint Thumbprints
- Anise Snowflake Cookies
- Pecan Sandies
- Cinnamon Roll Cookies
- Butterscotch Oatmeal Cookies
- Cardamom Crescent Cookies
- Coconut Macaroons
- Chocolate Cherry Cookies
- Mexican Wedding Cookies
- Hazelnut Linzer Cookies
- M&M Christmas Cookies
- Snowball Cookies (Russian Tea Cakes)
- Candy Cane Cookies
- Amaretti Cookies
- Apricot Kolaches
- Fig Newtons
- Cranberry Pistachio Shortbread
- Lemon Lavender Cookies
- Maple Pecan Cookies
- Chocolate Hazelnut Biscotti
- Orange Cardamom Cookies

- Brown Butter Snickerdoodles
- Raspberry Almond Thumbprint Cookies
- Chocolate Toffee Cookies
- Molasses Crinkle Cookies
- Matcha White Chocolate Cookies
- Peanut Butter Blossoms
- Chocolate Dipped Coconut Macaroons
- Cherry Chocolate Chip Cookies
- Oatmeal Raisin Cookies
- Brownie Cookies
- Espresso Chocolate Shortbread
- Lemon Poppy Seed Cookies
- Fig and Walnut Rugelach
- Chocolate Cherry Blossoms
- Chocolate Gingerbread Cookies

Classic Sugar Cookies

Ingredients:

- 2 3/4 cups all-purpose flour
- 1 teaspoon baking soda
- 1/2 teaspoon baking powder
- 1 cup unsalted butter, softened
- 1 1/2 cups granulated sugar
- 1 large egg
- 2 teaspoons vanilla extract
- Additional sugar for rolling (optional)

Instructions:

Preheat Oven: Preheat your oven to 375°F (190°C) and line baking sheets with parchment paper or silicone mats.
Combine Dry Ingredients: In a medium bowl, whisk together the flour, baking soda, and baking powder. Set aside.
Cream Butter and Sugar: In a large mixing bowl, beat together the softened butter and granulated sugar until light and fluffy, about 2-3 minutes.
Add Egg and Vanilla: Beat in the egg and vanilla extract until well combined.
Mix in Dry Ingredients: Gradually add the dry ingredient mixture to the wet ingredients, mixing until just combined. Be careful not to overmix.
Chill Dough (Optional): If the dough is too soft to roll, you can chill it in the refrigerator for about 30 minutes.
Roll and Cut: On a lightly floured surface, roll out the dough to about 1/4-inch thickness. Use cookie cutters to cut out desired shapes.
Place on Baking Sheets: Transfer the cut-out cookies to the prepared baking sheets, spacing them about 2 inches apart.
Optional Sugar Coating: If desired, sprinkle the tops of the cookies with granulated sugar before baking.
Bake: Bake in the preheated oven for 8-10 minutes or until the edges are just beginning to turn golden.
Cool: Allow the cookies to cool on the baking sheets for a few minutes before transferring them to wire racks to cool completely.
Decorate (Optional): Once cooled, decorate the cookies with icing, sprinkles, or other decorations as desired.

Enjoy these classic sugar cookies as-is or get creative with your favorite frosting and decorations for festive holiday treats!

Gingerbread Cookies

Ingredients:

- 3 cups all-purpose flour
- 1 teaspoon baking soda
- 1/4 teaspoon salt
- 1 tablespoon ground ginger
- 1 1/2 teaspoons ground cinnamon
- 1/2 teaspoon ground cloves
- 1/2 teaspoon ground nutmeg
- 3/4 cup unsalted butter, softened
- 1/2 cup packed brown sugar
- 1/2 cup granulated sugar
- 1/2 cup molasses
- 1 large egg
- 1 teaspoon vanilla extract

Instructions:

Preheat Oven: Preheat your oven to 350°F (175°C). Line baking sheets with parchment paper or silicone mats.

Combine Dry Ingredients: In a medium bowl, whisk together the flour, baking soda, salt, ginger, cinnamon, cloves, and nutmeg. Set aside.

Cream Butter and Sugars: In a large mixing bowl, beat together the softened butter, brown sugar, and granulated sugar until light and fluffy.

Add Molasses, Egg, and Vanilla: Beat in the molasses, egg, and vanilla extract until well combined.

Mix in Dry Ingredients: Gradually add the dry ingredient mixture to the wet ingredients, mixing until a dough forms.

Chill Dough: Wrap the dough in plastic wrap and refrigerate for at least 1 hour or until firm.

Roll and Cut: On a lightly floured surface, roll out the chilled dough to about 1/4-inch thickness. Use cookie cutters to cut out desired shapes.

Place on Baking Sheets: Transfer the cut-out cookies to the prepared baking sheets, spacing them about 1 inch apart.

Bake: Bake in the preheated oven for 8-10 minutes or until the edges are set and just beginning to brown.

Cool: Allow the cookies to cool on the baking sheets for a few minutes before transferring them to wire racks to cool completely.

Decorate (Optional): Once cooled, decorate the gingerbread cookies with icing, candies, or other decorations as desired.

These classic gingerbread cookies are perfect for holiday gatherings and can be decorated with royal icing for a festive touch! Enjoy the spicy-sweet flavors of these delightful treats.

Peppermint Chocolate Crinkle Cookies

Ingredients:

- 1 cup all-purpose flour
- 1/2 cup unsweetened cocoa powder
- 1 teaspoon baking powder
- 1/4 teaspoon salt
- 1 cup granulated sugar
- 1/4 cup vegetable oil
- 2 large eggs
- 1 teaspoon vanilla extract
- 1/2 teaspoon peppermint extract
- 1/2 cup powdered sugar
- Crushed candy canes or peppermint candies, for topping (optional)

Instructions:

Preheat Oven: Preheat your oven to 350°F (175°C). Line baking sheets with parchment paper or silicone mats.

Combine Dry Ingredients: In a medium bowl, whisk together the flour, cocoa powder, baking powder, and salt. Set aside.

Mix Wet Ingredients: In a large mixing bowl, whisk together the granulated sugar and vegetable oil until well combined. Add the eggs, vanilla extract, and peppermint extract, and whisk until smooth.

Combine Dry and Wet Mixtures: Gradually add the dry ingredient mixture to the wet ingredients, stirring until just combined. The dough will be soft and slightly sticky.

Chill Dough (Optional): If the dough is too soft to handle, cover and refrigerate for about 30 minutes until firm enough to roll into balls.

Form Cookie Balls: Place the powdered sugar in a shallow bowl. Scoop out tablespoon-sized portions of dough and roll them into balls. Roll each ball in the powdered sugar until coated all over.

Place on Baking Sheets: Arrange the coated cookie balls on the prepared baking sheets, spacing them about 2 inches apart.

Bake: Bake in the preheated oven for 10-12 minutes. The cookies will spread and crackle on top.

Top with Crushed Peppermint (Optional): If desired, immediately sprinkle the tops of the warm cookies with crushed candy canes or peppermint candies.

Cool and Serve: Allow the cookies to cool on the baking sheets for a few minutes, then transfer them to wire racks to cool completely.

Store: Store the cookies in an airtight container at room temperature for up to a week. Enjoy the festive peppermint chocolate flavor!

These Peppermint Chocolate Crinkle Cookies are perfect for holiday parties or as gifts. The combination of rich chocolate and refreshing peppermint is a delightful treat during the festive season.

Snickerdoodles

Ingredients:

- 2 3/4 cups all-purpose flour
- 2 teaspoons cream of tartar
- 1 teaspoon baking soda
- 1/4 teaspoon salt
- 1 cup unsalted butter, softened
- 1 1/2 cups granulated sugar
- 2 large eggs
- 1 teaspoon vanilla extract

For Rolling:

- 1/4 cup granulated sugar
- 1 tablespoon ground cinnamon

Instructions:

Preheat Oven: Preheat your oven to 375°F (190°C). Line baking sheets with parchment paper or silicone mats.
Mix Dry Ingredients: In a medium bowl, whisk together the flour, cream of tartar, baking soda, and salt. Set aside.
Cream Butter and Sugar: In a large mixing bowl, beat together the softened butter and 1 1/2 cups granulated sugar until light and fluffy.
Add Eggs and Vanilla: Beat in the eggs and vanilla extract until well combined.
Combine Wet and Dry Mixtures: Gradually add the dry ingredient mixture to the wet ingredients, mixing until just combined. Do not overmix.
Chill Dough (Optional): If the dough is too soft, cover and refrigerate for about 30 minutes to firm it up.
Make Cinnamon Sugar Mixture: In a small bowl, mix together 1/4 cup granulated sugar and 1 tablespoon ground cinnamon.
Form Dough Balls: Shape the dough into 1-inch balls, then roll each ball in the cinnamon sugar mixture until coated all over.
Place on Baking Sheets: Arrange the coated dough balls on the prepared baking sheets, spacing them about 2 inches apart.

Flatten (Optional): For slightly crispier cookies, gently flatten each dough ball with the bottom of a glass.

Bake: Bake in the preheated oven for 10-12 minutes or until the edges are set and just beginning to brown.

Cool and Serve: Allow the cookies to cool on the baking sheets for a few minutes, then transfer them to wire racks to cool completely.

Store: Store the Snickerdoodles in an airtight container at room temperature for several days. Enjoy these classic cinnamon-sugar cookies with a cup of milk or hot cocoa!

These Snickerdoodles are a beloved holiday treat with their soft and chewy texture and delightful cinnamon-sugar coating. They're perfect for cookie exchanges and festive gatherings. Enjoy baking and sharing these delicious cookies!

Linzer Cookies

Ingredients:

- 1 cup unsalted butter, softened
- 3/4 cup granulated sugar
- 1 large egg
- 1 teaspoon vanilla extract
- 2 cups all-purpose flour
- 1/2 teaspoon ground cinnamon
- 1/4 teaspoon salt
- 1 cup almond flour (or finely ground almonds)
- 1/2 cup raspberry or strawberry jam
- Powdered sugar, for dusting

Instructions:

Preheat Oven: Preheat your oven to 350°F (175°C). Line baking sheets with parchment paper or silicone mats.

Cream Butter and Sugar: In a large mixing bowl, beat together the softened butter and granulated sugar until light and fluffy.

Add Egg and Vanilla: Beat in the egg and vanilla extract until well combined.

Combine Dry Ingredients: In a separate bowl, whisk together the all-purpose flour, ground cinnamon, salt, and almond flour.

Mix Wet and Dry Ingredients: Gradually add the dry ingredient mixture to the wet ingredients, mixing until a dough forms. Divide the dough in half, shape into discs, wrap in plastic wrap, and refrigerate for at least 1 hour or until firm.

Roll Out Dough: On a lightly floured surface, roll out one disc of chilled dough to about 1/4-inch thickness. Use a round cookie cutter (about 2 inches in diameter) to cut out cookies. Use a smaller cookie cutter (such as a heart or star shape) to cut out the centers of half of the cookies. Repeat with the second disc of dough.

Bake: Place the cookies on the prepared baking sheets and bake for 10-12 minutes or until the edges are lightly golden. Let the cookies cool on the baking sheets for a few minutes before transferring them to wire racks to cool completely.

Assemble Linzer Cookies: Spread a thin layer of jam on the solid cookies (cookies without holes). Place a cut-out cookie on top of each jam-coated cookie to create a sandwich. Lightly dust the tops of the cookies with powdered sugar.

Serve: These Linzer Cookies are best enjoyed once assembled and allowed to set for a bit. They are perfect for holiday gatherings and can be stored in an airtight container at room temperature for a few days.

These delightful Linzer Cookies are a classic holiday treat with their buttery almond flavor and sweet fruity filling. They make a beautiful addition to any cookie platter or dessert table during the festive season!

Thumbprint Cookies (with assorted jams)

Ingredients:

- 1 cup unsalted butter, softened
- 2/3 cup granulated sugar
- 1/2 teaspoon vanilla extract
- 2 cups all-purpose flour
- Assorted jams or preserves (such as raspberry, strawberry, apricot, or any favorite flavor)
- Powdered sugar, for dusting (optional)

Instructions:

Preheat Oven: Preheat your oven to 350°F (175°C). Line baking sheets with parchment paper or silicone mats.
Cream Butter and Sugar: In a large mixing bowl, beat together the softened butter and granulated sugar until light and fluffy.
Add Vanilla and Flour: Beat in the vanilla extract. Gradually add the flour, mixing until a dough forms.
Form Dough Balls: Shape the dough into 1-inch balls and place them on the prepared baking sheets, spacing them about 1 inch apart.
Make Thumbprints: Use your thumb or the back of a small spoon to make an indentation in the center of each dough ball.
Fill with Jam: Spoon a small amount (about 1/2 teaspoon) of jam or preserves into each indentation. You can use a single flavor of jam or create a variety by using different flavors.
Bake: Bake in the preheated oven for 10-12 minutes or until the edges are just beginning to turn golden.
Cool and Dust with Powdered Sugar: Allow the cookies to cool on the baking sheets for a few minutes before transferring them to wire racks to cool completely. Once cooled, dust the tops of the cookies with powdered sugar, if desired.
Serve: These Thumbprint Cookies are best enjoyed once cooled and the jam has set. They are perfect for holiday cookie platters or as sweet treats throughout the year.

These Thumbprint Cookies are versatile and can be customized with your favorite jams or preserves. They have a buttery, melt-in-your-mouth texture and are sure to be a hit at any gathering!

White Chocolate Macadamia Nut Cookies

Ingredients:

- 1 cup unsalted butter, softened
- 1 cup granulated sugar
- 1 cup light brown sugar, packed
- 2 large eggs
- 1 teaspoon vanilla extract
- 2 1/2 cups all-purpose flour
- 1 teaspoon baking soda
- 1/2 teaspoon salt
- 1 cup white chocolate chips or chunks
- 1 cup macadamia nuts, coarsely chopped

Instructions:

Preheat Oven: Preheat your oven to 350°F (175°C). Line baking sheets with parchment paper or silicone mats.

Cream Butter and Sugars: In a large mixing bowl, beat together the softened butter, granulated sugar, and brown sugar until light and fluffy.

Add Eggs and Vanilla: Beat in the eggs, one at a time, until well combined. Add the vanilla extract and mix until smooth.

Combine Dry Ingredients: In a separate bowl, whisk together the flour, baking soda, and salt.

Mix Wet and Dry Ingredients: Gradually add the dry ingredient mixture to the wet ingredients, mixing until just combined.

Stir in Chocolate and Nuts: Fold in the white chocolate chips or chunks and chopped macadamia nuts until evenly distributed in the dough.

Form Dough Balls: Drop tablespoon-sized portions of dough onto the prepared baking sheets, spacing them about 2 inches apart.

Bake: Bake in the preheated oven for 10-12 minutes or until the edges are golden brown.

Cool and Serve: Allow the cookies to cool on the baking sheets for a few minutes before transferring them to wire racks to cool completely.

Enjoy: These White Chocolate Macadamia Nut Cookies are best enjoyed warm or at room temperature with a glass of milk or cup of coffee. Store any leftovers in an airtight container.

These cookies are a delicious combination of sweet white chocolate and rich macadamia nuts, perfect for satisfying your sweet tooth. They are great for holidays, parties, or anytime you crave a delightful homemade treat!

Chocolate-Dipped Shortbread Cookies

Ingredients:

- 1 cup unsalted butter, softened
- 1/2 cup granulated sugar
- 2 cups all-purpose flour
- 1/4 teaspoon salt
- 1 teaspoon vanilla extract
- 6 ounces semi-sweet or dark chocolate, chopped
- Optional: Sprinkles, chopped nuts, or sea salt for topping

Instructions:

Preheat Oven: Preheat your oven to 350°F (175°C). Line baking sheets with parchment paper or silicone mats.

Cream Butter and Sugar: In a large mixing bowl, beat together the softened butter and granulated sugar until light and fluffy.

Add Vanilla and Dry Ingredients: Add the vanilla extract, flour, and salt to the bowl. Mix until a dough forms. The dough will be crumbly but should stick together when pressed.

Shape Dough: Gather the dough into a ball and knead briefly until smooth. Roll out the dough on a lightly floured surface to about 1/4-inch thickness.

Cut into Shapes: Use cookie cutters to cut out shapes (such as rounds or rectangles) and place them on the prepared baking sheets.

Bake: Bake in the preheated oven for 12-15 minutes or until the edges are just beginning to turn golden. The cookies should be firm but not browned.

Cool: Allow the cookies to cool on the baking sheets for a few minutes before transferring them to wire racks to cool completely.

Melt Chocolate: In a microwave-safe bowl or using a double boiler, melt the chopped chocolate until smooth and glossy.

Dip Cookies: Dip each cooled shortbread cookie halfway into the melted chocolate, allowing any excess chocolate to drip off.

Decorate (Optional): Immediately sprinkle the dipped portion of the cookies with sprinkles, chopped nuts, or a pinch of sea salt while the chocolate is still wet.

Set Chocolate: Place the dipped cookies on a parchment-lined tray and allow the chocolate to set at room temperature. You can also place them in the refrigerator for faster setting.

Serve and Enjoy: Once the chocolate is set, these delicious Chocolate-Dipped Shortbread Cookies are ready to be enjoyed! Store any leftovers in an airtight container.

These cookies are a delightful combination of buttery shortbread and rich chocolate, perfect for holiday gatherings, afternoon tea, or as a sweet treat any time of the year. Customize them with your favorite toppings and enjoy!

Cranberry Orange Biscotti

Ingredients:

- 2 cups all-purpose flour
- 1 cup granulated sugar
- 1 teaspoon baking powder
- 1/2 teaspoon baking soda
- 1/4 teaspoon salt
- Zest of 1 orange
- 1/2 cup unsalted butter, softened
- 2 large eggs
- 1 teaspoon vanilla extract
- 1 cup dried cranberries
- 1/2 cup chopped almonds or walnuts (optional)
- 1/2 cup white chocolate chips or chunks (optional, for drizzling)

Instructions:

Preheat Oven: Preheat your oven to 350°F (175°C). Line a baking sheet with parchment paper or a silicone mat.

Mix Dry Ingredients: In a medium bowl, whisk together the flour, sugar, baking powder, baking soda, salt, and orange zest.

Combine Wet Ingredients: In a large mixing bowl, cream together the softened butter, eggs, and vanilla extract until well combined.

Combine Wet and Dry Mixtures: Gradually add the dry ingredient mixture to the wet ingredients, mixing until a dough forms. Fold in the dried cranberries and chopped nuts (if using).

Shape Dough: Divide the dough in half. On a lightly floured surface, shape each half into a log about 12 inches long and 2 inches wide. Place the logs on the prepared baking sheet, spacing them apart.

Bake First Time: Bake in the preheated oven for 25 minutes or until the logs are firm and just beginning to turn golden brown. Remove from the oven and let cool for 10 minutes.

Slice Biscotti: Using a sharp knife, slice the logs diagonally into 1/2-inch thick slices. Place the slices cut-side down on the baking sheet.

Bake Again: Return the biscotti slices to the oven and bake for an additional 10-12 minutes, flipping the slices halfway through baking, until the biscotti are golden and crisp.

Cool Completely: Remove the biscotti from the oven and let cool completely on wire racks.

Optional White Chocolate Drizzle: Melt the white chocolate chips or chunks in the microwave or using a double boiler until smooth. Drizzle the melted chocolate over the cooled biscotti.

Set Chocolate (if using): Let the chocolate set before serving or storing the biscotti.

Serve and Enjoy: These Cranberry Orange Biscotti are perfect for dipping in coffee, tea, or hot chocolate. Store in an airtight container at room temperature for up to two weeks.

These biscotti have a wonderful combination of tart cranberries, citrusy orange zest, and crunchy nuts, making them a delightful holiday treat or anytime snack. Enjoy baking and savoring these delicious cookies!

Red Velvet Crinkle Cookies

Ingredients:

- 1 3/4 cups all-purpose flour
- 1/4 cup unsweetened cocoa powder
- 1 1/2 teaspoons baking powder
- 1/4 teaspoon salt
- 1/2 cup unsalted butter, softened
- 1 cup granulated sugar
- 2 large eggs
- 2 teaspoons vanilla extract
- 1 tablespoon red food coloring (gel or liquid)
- 1 cup powdered sugar, for rolling

Instructions:

Preheat Oven: Preheat your oven to 350°F (175°C). Line baking sheets with parchment paper or silicone mats.

Mix Dry Ingredients: In a medium bowl, whisk together the flour, cocoa powder, baking powder, and salt. Set aside.

Cream Butter and Sugar: In a large mixing bowl, beat together the softened butter and granulated sugar until light and fluffy.

Add Eggs, Vanilla, and Food Coloring: Beat in the eggs, one at a time, followed by the vanilla extract and red food coloring. Mix until well combined.

Combine Wet and Dry Mixtures: Gradually add the dry ingredient mixture to the wet ingredients, mixing until just combined. The dough will be thick and slightly sticky.

Chill Dough (Optional): If the dough is too soft to handle, cover and refrigerate for about 30 minutes.

Roll Dough into Balls: Scoop tablespoon-sized portions of dough and roll them into balls using your hands.

Roll in Powdered Sugar: Roll each dough ball generously in powdered sugar until coated all over.

Place on Baking Sheets: Arrange the coated dough balls on the prepared baking sheets, spacing them about 2 inches apart.

Bake: Bake in the preheated oven for 10-12 minutes or until the cookies have cracked and are set around the edges.

Cool and Serve: Allow the cookies to cool on the baking sheets for a few minutes before transferring them to wire racks to cool completely.

Enjoy: These Red Velvet Crinkle Cookies are perfect for holiday celebrations or anytime you're craving a festive and delicious treat!

These cookies have a rich chocolatey flavor with a hint of tanginess from the cream cheese, and they look beautiful with their crackled red appearance. They're sure to be a hit at parties or as homemade gifts during the holiday season!

Almond Butter Cookies

Ingredients:

- 1 cup almond butter (creamy or crunchy)
- 1/2 cup granulated sugar
- 1/2 cup packed light brown sugar
- 1 large egg
- 1 teaspoon vanilla extract
- 1/2 teaspoon baking soda
- 1/4 teaspoon salt
- Optional: Sliced almonds for topping

Instructions:

Preheat Oven: Preheat your oven to 350°F (175°C). Line baking sheets with parchment paper or silicone mats.

Mix Wet Ingredients: In a large mixing bowl, combine the almond butter, granulated sugar, and brown sugar. Mix until well combined and smooth.

Add Egg and Vanilla: Add the egg and vanilla extract to the almond butter mixture, and mix until fully incorporated.

Add Baking Soda and Salt: Sprinkle the baking soda and salt over the mixture, and mix until evenly distributed.

Form Dough Balls: Scoop tablespoon-sized portions of dough and roll them into balls using your hands. Place the dough balls on the prepared baking sheets, spacing them about 2 inches apart.

Flatten Dough Balls (Optional): Use a fork to gently press down on each dough ball to create a criss-cross pattern. Alternatively, flatten the dough balls slightly with the palm of your hand.

Top with Sliced Almonds (Optional): If desired, gently press a few sliced almonds onto the tops of the cookies for decoration and added crunch.

Bake: Bake in the preheated oven for 10-12 minutes or until the edges are lightly golden.

Cool and Serve: Allow the cookies to cool on the baking sheets for a few minutes before transferring them to wire racks to cool completely.

Enjoy: These Almond Butter Cookies are deliciously nutty and make a wonderful gluten-free treat. They're perfect for enjoying with a cup of tea or coffee!

These almond butter cookies are simple to make and have a delightful almond flavor. They're great for anyone looking for a gluten-free cookie option or simply loves the taste of almonds. Enjoy baking and savoring these delicious treats!

Lemon Glazed Cookies

Ingredients:

For the Cookies:

- 2 cups all-purpose flour
- 1/2 teaspoon baking powder
- 1/4 teaspoon salt
- 1/2 cup unsalted butter, softened
- 1 cup granulated sugar
- 1 large egg
- 1 teaspoon vanilla extract
- Zest of 1 lemon
- 2 tablespoons fresh lemon juice

For the Glaze:

- 1 cup powdered sugar
- 2-3 tablespoons fresh lemon juice
- Zest of 1 lemon (optional, for garnish)

Instructions:

Preheat Oven: Preheat your oven to 350°F (175°C). Line baking sheets with parchment paper or silicone mats.

Mix Dry Ingredients: In a medium bowl, whisk together the flour, baking powder, and salt. Set aside.

Cream Butter and Sugar: In a large mixing bowl, beat together the softened butter and granulated sugar until light and fluffy.

Add Egg, Vanilla, Lemon Zest, and Juice: Beat in the egg until well combined. Add the vanilla extract, lemon zest, and lemon juice, and mix until incorporated.

Combine Wet and Dry Mixtures: Gradually add the dry ingredient mixture to the wet ingredients, mixing until just combined and a dough forms.

Shape Dough: Drop tablespoon-sized portions of dough onto the prepared baking sheets, spacing them about 2 inches apart. Flatten the dough slightly with the back of a spoon or your fingertips.

Bake: Bake in the preheated oven for 10-12 minutes or until the edges are just beginning to turn golden. Remove from the oven and let the cookies cool on the baking sheets for a few minutes before transferring them to wire racks to cool completely.

Prepare Glaze: In a small bowl, whisk together the powdered sugar and fresh lemon juice until smooth and combined. Adjust the consistency by adding more lemon juice (for a thinner glaze) or powdered sugar (for a thicker glaze).

Glaze the Cookies: Once the cookies are completely cooled, drizzle the lemon glaze over the tops of the cookies using a spoon or fork. Allow the glaze to set for a few minutes.

Garnish (Optional): Sprinkle additional lemon zest over the glazed cookies for extra lemon flavor and a decorative touch.

Serve and Enjoy: These Lemon Glazed Cookies are bright, zesty, and perfect for citrus lovers. They make a delightful treat for any occasion!

These lemon glazed cookies are refreshing and bursting with citrus flavor. They are great for serving at parties, brunches, or as a sweet snack with tea. Enjoy baking these delicious cookies and sharing them with family and friends!

Eggnog Cookies

Ingredients:

For the Cookies:

- 2 1/4 cups all-purpose flour
- 1 teaspoon baking powder
- 1/2 teaspoon ground nutmeg
- 1/2 teaspoon ground cinnamon
- 1/4 teaspoon salt
- 1/2 cup unsalted butter, softened
- 1 cup granulated sugar
- 1/2 cup eggnog
- 1 teaspoon vanilla extract
- 2 large egg yolks

For the Glaze:

- 1 1/2 cups powdered sugar
- 3-4 tablespoons eggnog
- Ground nutmeg, for sprinkling (optional)

Instructions:

Preheat Oven: Preheat your oven to 350°F (175°C). Line baking sheets with parchment paper or silicone mats.

Mix Dry Ingredients: In a medium bowl, whisk together the flour, baking powder, ground nutmeg, ground cinnamon, and salt. Set aside.

Cream Butter and Sugar: In a large mixing bowl, beat together the softened butter and granulated sugar until light and fluffy.

Add Eggnog, Vanilla, and Egg Yolks: Mix in the eggnog, vanilla extract, and egg yolks until well combined.

Combine Wet and Dry Mixtures: Gradually add the dry ingredient mixture to the wet ingredients, mixing until a soft dough forms.

Shape Dough: Drop tablespoon-sized portions of dough onto the prepared baking sheets, spacing them about 2 inches apart.

Flatten Dough Balls (Optional): Flatten the dough balls slightly with the back of a spoon or your fingertips.

Bake: Bake in the preheated oven for 10-12 minutes or until the edges are just beginning to turn golden. Remove from the oven and let the cookies cool on the baking sheets for a few minutes before transferring them to wire racks to cool completely.

Prepare Glaze: In a small bowl, whisk together the powdered sugar and eggnog until smooth and combined. Adjust the consistency by adding more eggnog (for a thinner glaze) or powdered sugar (for a thicker glaze).

Glaze the Cookies: Once the cookies are completely cooled, drizzle the eggnog glaze over the tops of the cookies using a spoon or fork.

Sprinkle with Nutmeg (Optional): Sprinkle ground nutmeg over the glazed cookies for extra flavor and a decorative touch.

Serve and Enjoy: These Eggnog Cookies are festive and perfect for the holiday season. They pair wonderfully with a cup of eggnog or hot cocoa!

These eggnog cookies capture the delicious flavors of traditional eggnog in a delightful cookie form. Enjoy baking and sharing these festive treats with friends and family during the holidays!

Pistachio Cranberry Biscotti

Ingredients:

- 2 cups all-purpose flour
- 1 1/2 teaspoons baking powder
- 1/4 teaspoon salt
- 3/4 cup granulated sugar
- 1/2 cup unsalted butter, melted and cooled slightly
- 2 large eggs
- 1 teaspoon vanilla extract
- 1/2 cup shelled pistachios, coarsely chopped
- 1/2 cup dried cranberries

For Optional Drizzle:

- 4 ounces white chocolate, melted (optional)

Instructions:

Preheat Oven: Preheat your oven to 350°F (175°C). Line a baking sheet with parchment paper.

Mix Dry Ingredients: In a medium bowl, whisk together the flour, baking powder, and salt. Set aside.

Combine Wet Ingredients: In a large mixing bowl, whisk together the sugar, melted butter, eggs, and vanilla extract until smooth.

Mix in Dry Ingredients: Gradually add the dry ingredient mixture to the wet ingredients, stirring until just combined.

Add Pistachios and Cranberries: Fold in the chopped pistachios and dried cranberries until evenly distributed in the dough.

Shape Dough: Divide the dough in half. On a lightly floured surface, shape each half into a log about 12 inches long and 2 inches wide. Place the logs on the prepared baking sheet, spacing them apart.

Bake First Time: Bake in the preheated oven for 25-30 minutes or until the logs are firm and just beginning to turn golden. Remove from the oven and let cool for 10 minutes.

Slice Biscotti: Using a sharp knife, slice the logs diagonally into 1/2-inch thick slices. Place the slices cut-side down on the baking sheet.

Bake Again: Return the biscotti slices to the oven and bake for an additional 10-12 minutes, flipping the slices halfway through baking, until the biscotti are golden and crisp.

Optional Drizzle: Once the biscotti are completely cooled, drizzle melted white chocolate over the tops of the biscotti for decoration and added sweetness.

Cool and Serve: Allow the biscotti to cool completely on wire racks before serving or storing in an airtight container.

Enjoy: These Pistachio Cranberry Biscotti are perfect for dipping into coffee, tea, or hot chocolate. They also make lovely homemade gifts during the holiday season!

These biscotti are crunchy, flavorful, and perfect for enjoying with a warm beverage. The combination of pistachios and cranberries gives them a festive and delicious twist. Enjoy baking and savoring these delightful treats!

Chocolate Peppermint Thumbprints

Ingredients:

- 1 cup all-purpose flour
- 1/3 cup unsweetened cocoa powder
- 1/4 teaspoon salt
- 1/2 cup unsalted butter, softened
- 2/3 cup granulated sugar
- 1 large egg, separated
- 2 tablespoons milk
- 1 teaspoon vanilla extract
- 1 cup semi-sweet or dark chocolate chips
- 1/2 teaspoon peppermint extract
- Crushed peppermint candies or candy canes, for topping

Instructions:

Preheat Oven: Preheat your oven to 350°F (175°C). Line baking sheets with parchment paper or silicone mats.

Mix Dry Ingredients: In a medium bowl, whisk together the flour, cocoa powder, and salt. Set aside.

Cream Butter and Sugar: In a large mixing bowl, beat together the softened butter and granulated sugar until light and fluffy.

Add Egg Yolk, Milk, and Vanilla: Add the egg yolk, milk, and vanilla extract to the butter mixture, and beat until well combined.

Combine Wet and Dry Mixtures: Gradually add the dry ingredient mixture to the wet ingredients, mixing until a dough forms.

Shape Dough into Balls: Roll tablespoon-sized portions of dough into balls and place them on the prepared baking sheets, spacing them about 1 inch apart.

Make Thumbprints: Use your thumb or the back of a spoon to gently press down in the center of each dough ball to create a small indentation.

Bake: Bake in the preheated oven for 10-12 minutes. Remove from the oven and let the cookies cool on the baking sheets for a few minutes before transferring them to wire racks to cool completely.

Prepare Peppermint Chocolate Filling: In a microwave-safe bowl, melt the chocolate chips in 30-second intervals, stirring in between, until smooth. Stir in the peppermint extract.

Fill Cookies: Spoon a small amount of the melted chocolate-peppermint mixture into the center of each cookie, filling the indentations.
Top with Crushed Peppermint: Sprinkle crushed peppermint candies or candy canes over the melted chocolate filling before it sets.
Let Set: Allow the cookies to cool completely until the chocolate filling has set.
Serve and Enjoy: These Chocolate Peppermint Thumbprint Cookies are a delightful holiday treat with a perfect combination of chocolate and peppermint flavors!

These cookies are perfect for holiday gatherings, cookie exchanges, or as a special treat for yourself. The rich chocolate cookie base with a refreshing peppermint filling and crunchy candy topping is sure to be a hit. Enjoy making and sharing these delicious cookies!

Anise Snowflake Cookies

Ingredients:

- 2 cups all-purpose flour
- 1/2 teaspoon baking powder
- 1/4 teaspoon salt
- 1/2 cup unsalted butter, softened
- 1 cup granulated sugar
- 2 large eggs
- 1 teaspoon anise extract
- 1/2 teaspoon vanilla extract
- Powdered sugar, for dusting

Instructions:

Preheat Oven: Preheat your oven to 375°F (190°C). Line baking sheets with parchment paper or silicone mats.
Mix Dry Ingredients: In a medium bowl, whisk together the flour, baking powder, and salt. Set aside.
Cream Butter and Sugar: In a large mixing bowl, beat together the softened butter and granulated sugar until light and fluffy.
Add Eggs and Extracts: Beat in the eggs, one at a time, until well combined. Add the anise extract and vanilla extract, and mix until incorporated.
Combine Wet and Dry Mixtures: Gradually add the dry ingredient mixture to the wet ingredients, mixing until a dough forms.
Chill Dough (Optional): If the dough is too soft to handle, cover and refrigerate for about 30 minutes.
Roll and Cut Dough: On a lightly floured surface, roll out the dough to about 1/4-inch thickness. Use snowflake-shaped cookie cutters to cut out cookies. Place the cut-out cookies on the prepared baking sheets, spacing them about 1 inch apart.
Bake: Bake in the preheated oven for 8-10 minutes or until the edges are just beginning to turn golden.
Cool and Dust with Powdered Sugar: Allow the cookies to cool on the baking sheets for a few minutes, then transfer them to wire racks to cool completely. Dust the cooled cookies with powdered sugar using a fine-mesh sieve.

Serve and Enjoy: These Anise Snowflake Cookies are delicate and aromatic, perfect for winter and holiday celebrations. They pair wonderfully with a cup of tea or coffee!

These cookies have a unique flavor from the anise extract and a beautiful snowflake shape, making them a lovely addition to any cookie platter. Enjoy baking and decorating these delightful Anise Snowflake Cookies for festive occasions!

Pecan Sandies

Ingredients:

- 1 cup unsalted butter, softened
- 1/2 cup granulated sugar
- 2 teaspoons vanilla extract
- 2 cups all-purpose flour
- 1 cup pecans, finely chopped
- Powdered sugar, for dusting

Instructions:

Preheat Oven: Preheat your oven to 350°F (175°C). Line baking sheets with parchment paper or silicone mats.
Cream Butter and Sugar: In a large mixing bowl, beat together the softened butter and granulated sugar until light and fluffy.
Add Vanilla and Flour: Mix in the vanilla extract. Gradually add the flour, mixing until well combined.
Fold in Pecans: Gently fold in the finely chopped pecans until evenly distributed in the dough.
Shape Dough into Balls: Roll tablespoon-sized portions of dough into balls and place them on the prepared baking sheets, spacing them about 1 inch apart.
Flatten Dough Balls: Use the bottom of a glass or a fork to gently flatten each dough ball to about 1/2-inch thickness.
Bake: Bake in the preheated oven for 12-15 minutes or until the edges are lightly golden.
Cool and Dust with Powdered Sugar: Allow the cookies to cool on the baking sheets for a few minutes before transferring them to wire racks to cool completely. Dust the cooled cookies generously with powdered sugar.
Serve and Enjoy: These Pecan Sandies are buttery, nutty, and deliciously crumbly. They are perfect for enjoying with a cup of coffee or tea!

These classic Pecan Sandies are a wonderful treat for any occasion, and they also make a great homemade gift during the holiday season. Enjoy making and savoring these delightful cookies with their rich pecan flavor and sandy texture!

Cinnamon Roll Cookies

Ingredients:

For the Cookie Dough:

- 1 cup unsalted butter, softened
- 1 cup granulated sugar
- 2 large eggs
- 1 teaspoon vanilla extract
- 3 cups all-purpose flour
- 1/2 teaspoon salt

For the Cinnamon Filling:

- 1/2 cup unsalted butter, softened
- 1 cup packed light brown sugar
- 2 tablespoons ground cinnamon

For the Glaze:

- 1 cup powdered sugar
- 2-3 tablespoons milk or cream
- 1/2 teaspoon vanilla extract

Instructions:

Preheat Oven: Preheat your oven to 350°F (175°C). Line baking sheets with parchment paper or silicone mats.
Make Cookie Dough: In a large mixing bowl, cream together the softened butter and granulated sugar until light and fluffy. Add the eggs and vanilla extract, and mix until well combined. Gradually add the flour and salt, mixing until a dough forms.
Prepare Cinnamon Filling: In a separate bowl, mix together the softened butter, brown sugar, and ground cinnamon until smooth and well combined.
Roll Out Dough: Divide the cookie dough into two equal portions. On a lightly floured surface, roll out each portion into a rectangle about 1/4-inch thick.
Spread Cinnamon Filling: Spread half of the cinnamon filling evenly over each rectangle of dough, leaving a small border around the edges.

Roll Up Dough: Starting from one of the long sides, tightly roll up each rectangle of dough into a log, similar to rolling cinnamon rolls.

Chill Dough Logs (Optional): Wrap the dough logs in plastic wrap and chill in the refrigerator for at least 1 hour or until firm (this step helps with slicing).

Slice Dough: Using a sharp knife, slice each chilled dough log into 1/2-inch thick rounds. Place the rounds on the prepared baking sheets, spacing them about 2 inches apart.

Bake: Bake in the preheated oven for 10-12 minutes or until the edges are lightly golden.

Prepare Glaze: While the cookies are baking, prepare the glaze. In a small bowl, whisk together the powdered sugar, milk or cream, and vanilla extract until smooth.

Glaze Cookies: Remove the cookies from the oven and let them cool on the baking sheets for a few minutes. Drizzle the glaze over the warm cookies using a spoon or piping bag.

Serve and Enjoy: These Cinnamon Roll Cookies are a delightful twist on classic cinnamon rolls, perfect for enjoying with a cup of coffee or tea!

These cookies capture the flavors of cinnamon rolls in a portable and delicious treat. They are great for sharing during breakfast, brunch, or as a sweet snack any time of the day. Enjoy making and savoring these delightful Cinnamon Roll Cookies!

Butterscotch Oatmeal Cookies

Ingredients:

- 1 cup unsalted butter, softened
- 1 cup packed light brown sugar
- 1/2 cup granulated sugar
- 2 large eggs
- 1 teaspoon vanilla extract
- 1 1/2 cups all-purpose flour
- 1 teaspoon baking soda
- 1/2 teaspoon salt
- 3 cups old-fashioned rolled oats
- 1 1/2 cups butterscotch chips

Instructions:

Preheat Oven: Preheat your oven to 350°F (175°C). Line baking sheets with parchment paper or silicone mats.
Cream Butter and Sugars: In a large mixing bowl, cream together the softened butter, brown sugar, and granulated sugar until light and fluffy.
Add Eggs and Vanilla: Beat in the eggs, one at a time, until well combined. Add the vanilla extract and mix until incorporated.
Combine Dry Ingredients: In a separate bowl, whisk together the flour, baking soda, and salt.
Mix Wet and Dry Ingredients: Gradually add the dry ingredient mixture to the wet ingredients, mixing until just combined.
Fold in Oats and Butterscotch Chips: Stir in the rolled oats and butterscotch chips until evenly distributed in the dough.
Scoop Dough onto Baking Sheets: Drop rounded tablespoonfuls of dough onto the prepared baking sheets, spacing them about 2 inches apart.
Flatten Dough (Optional): Use the back of a spoon or your fingertips to gently flatten each dough mound.
Bake: Bake in the preheated oven for 10-12 minutes or until the edges are golden brown.
Cool and Serve: Allow the cookies to cool on the baking sheets for a few minutes before transferring them to wire racks to cool completely.

Enjoy: These Butterscotch Oatmeal Cookies are chewy, sweet, and loaded with butterscotch flavor. They are perfect for sharing with family and friends!

These cookies are a delightful combination of chewy oatmeal and rich butterscotch chips. They make a wonderful treat for parties, bake sales, or anytime you're craving a comforting cookie. Enjoy baking and savoring these Butterscotch Oatmeal Cookies!

Cardamom Crescent Cookies

Ingredients:

- 1 cup unsalted butter, softened
- 2/3 cup granulated sugar
- 2 teaspoons ground cardamom
- 1/2 teaspoon vanilla extract
- 2 cups all-purpose flour
- 1 cup almond flour (or finely ground almonds)
- 1/2 cup powdered sugar, for dusting

Instructions:

Preheat Oven: Preheat your oven to 350°F (175°C). Line baking sheets with parchment paper or silicone mats.
Cream Butter and Sugar: In a large mixing bowl, cream together the softened butter and granulated sugar until light and fluffy.
Add Cardamom and Vanilla: Mix in the ground cardamom and vanilla extract until well combined.
Add Flours: Gradually add the all-purpose flour and almond flour (or finely ground almonds) to the butter mixture, mixing until a dough forms. The dough should be smooth and slightly sticky.
Shape Dough: Take small portions of the dough and shape them into crescent shapes (small half-moons) or round cookies. Place them on the prepared baking sheets, spacing them about 1 inch apart.
Bake: Bake in the preheated oven for 12-15 minutes or until the cookies are just beginning to turn golden around the edges.
Cool and Dust with Powdered Sugar: Allow the cookies to cool on the baking sheets for a few minutes. While still slightly warm, dust the cookies generously with powdered sugar.
Serve and Enjoy: These Cardamom Crescent Cookies are delicate, buttery, and fragrant with cardamom flavor. They are perfect for serving with tea or coffee!

These cardamom-scented cookies are a delightful treat, especially during the holiday season. The aromatic flavor of cardamom pairs beautifully with the buttery texture of these cookies. Enjoy making and savoring these Cardamom Crescent Cookies with family and friends!

Coconut Macaroons

Ingredients:

- 4 large egg whites
- 1/2 cup granulated sugar
- 1/2 teaspoon vanilla extract
- 1/4 teaspoon almond extract (optional)
- 1/4 teaspoon salt
- 3 cups sweetened shredded coconut

Instructions:

Preheat Oven: Preheat your oven to 325°F (160°C). Line baking sheets with parchment paper or silicone mats.

Prepare Coconut Mixture: In a heatproof mixing bowl, whisk together the egg whites, sugar, vanilla extract, almond extract (if using), and salt.

Heat Mixture: Place the mixing bowl over a pot of simmering water (double boiler method). Whisk constantly until the mixture is warm to the touch and the sugar has dissolved (about 2-3 minutes).

Combine with Coconut: Remove the bowl from the heat and stir in the shredded coconut until well combined.

Form Macaroons: Using a spoon or cookie scoop, drop rounded tablespoons of the coconut mixture onto the prepared baking sheets, spacing them about 1 inch apart.

Bake: Bake in the preheated oven for 20-25 minutes or until the edges of the macaroons are golden brown.

Cool: Allow the macaroons to cool on the baking sheets for a few minutes, then transfer them to wire racks to cool completely.

Optional Chocolate Dip (if desired): Melt some chocolate chips (semi-sweet or dark) in the microwave or using a double boiler. Dip the bottoms of the cooled macaroons into the melted chocolate and place them back on the parchment paper to let the chocolate set.

Serve and Enjoy: These Coconut Macaroons are sweet, chewy, and wonderfully coconutty. They are perfect for dessert platters or as a sweet treat with coffee or tea!

These coconut macaroons are simple to make and always a hit with coconut lovers. Enjoy baking and savoring these delicious and chewy Coconut Macaroons!

Chocolate Cherry Cookies

Ingredients:

- 1 cup all-purpose flour
- 1/4 cup unsweetened cocoa powder
- 1/2 teaspoon baking powder
- 1/4 teaspoon salt
- 1/2 cup unsalted butter, softened
- 3/4 cup granulated sugar
- 1 large egg
- 1 teaspoon vanilla extract
- 1/2 cup semi-sweet chocolate chips
- 1/2 cup dried cherries, chopped

Instructions:

Preheat Oven: Preheat your oven to 350°F (175°C). Line baking sheets with parchment paper or silicone mats.

Mix Dry Ingredients: In a medium bowl, whisk together the flour, cocoa powder, baking powder, and salt. Set aside.

Cream Butter and Sugar: In a large mixing bowl, cream together the softened butter and granulated sugar until light and fluffy.

Add Egg and Vanilla: Beat in the egg and vanilla extract until well combined.

Combine Wet and Dry Mixtures: Gradually add the dry ingredient mixture to the wet ingredients, mixing until just combined.

Stir in Chocolate and Cherries: Fold in the chocolate chips and chopped dried cherries until evenly distributed in the dough.

Shape Dough into Balls: Drop tablespoon-sized portions of dough onto the prepared baking sheets, spacing them about 2 inches apart.

Flatten Dough Balls (Optional): Use the back of a spoon or your fingertips to gently flatten each dough ball.

Bake: Bake in the preheated oven for 10-12 minutes or until the edges are set.

Cool and Serve: Allow the cookies to cool on the baking sheets for a few minutes before transferring them to wire racks to cool completely.

Enjoy: These Chocolate Cherry Cookies are rich, chewy, and packed with delicious flavors. They are perfect for dessert or as a sweet snack!

These cookies are a delightful combination of chocolate and cherries, creating a perfect balance of sweetness and tartness. Enjoy baking and sharing these delicious Chocolate Cherry Cookies with your loved ones!

Mexican Wedding Cookies

Ingredients:

- 1 cup unsalted butter, softened
- 1/2 cup powdered sugar, plus more for coating
- 1 teaspoon vanilla extract
- 2 cups all-purpose flour
- 1 cup finely chopped pecans or walnuts

Instructions:

Preheat Oven: Preheat your oven to 350°F (175°C). Line baking sheets with parchment paper or silicone mats.
Cream Butter and Sugar: In a large mixing bowl, cream together the softened butter and powdered sugar until light and fluffy.
Add Vanilla and Flour: Mix in the vanilla extract. Gradually add the flour, mixing until just combined.
Stir in Chopped Nuts: Fold in the finely chopped pecans or walnuts until evenly distributed in the dough.
Shape Dough into Balls: Roll tablespoon-sized portions of dough into balls and place them on the prepared baking sheets, spacing them about 1 inch apart.
Bake: Bake in the preheated oven for 12-15 minutes or until the bottoms of the cookies are lightly golden.
Cool Slightly: Allow the cookies to cool on the baking sheets for a few minutes.
Coat with Powdered Sugar: While the cookies are still warm, gently roll them in powdered sugar to coat completely. Place the coated cookies on a wire rack to cool completely.
Re-Coat (Optional): If desired, once the cookies are completely cooled, roll them again in powdered sugar for a thicker coating.
Serve and Enjoy: These Mexican Wedding Cookies are buttery, nutty, and melt-in-your-mouth delicious! They are perfect for weddings, holidays, or any special occasion.

These cookies are a classic treat known for their delicate texture and sweet powdered sugar coating. They are easy to make and always a hit with friends and family. Enjoy baking and savoring these delightful Mexican Wedding Cookies!

Hazelnut Linzer Cookies

Ingredients:

- 1 cup hazelnuts, toasted and finely ground
- 2 cups all-purpose flour
- 1/2 teaspoon baking powder
- 1/4 teaspoon salt
- 1 cup unsalted butter, softened
- 3/4 cup granulated sugar
- 1 large egg
- 1 teaspoon vanilla extract
- Raspberry jam (or any preferred jam)
- Powdered sugar, for dusting

Instructions:

Prepare Hazelnuts: Preheat your oven to 350°F (175°C). Spread the hazelnuts on a baking sheet and toast them in the oven for about 8-10 minutes until lightly browned and fragrant. Allow the hazelnuts to cool, then remove the skins by rubbing them with a clean kitchen towel. Grind the hazelnuts in a food processor until finely ground.

Mix Dry Ingredients: In a medium bowl, whisk together the finely ground hazelnuts, flour, baking powder, and salt. Set aside.

Cream Butter and Sugar: In a large mixing bowl, cream together the softened butter and granulated sugar until light and fluffy.

Add Egg and Vanilla: Beat in the egg and vanilla extract until well combined.

Combine Wet and Dry Mixtures: Gradually add the dry ingredient mixture to the wet ingredients, mixing until a dough forms.

Chill Dough: Divide the dough into two equal portions, shape each portion into a disk, wrap them in plastic wrap, and refrigerate for at least 1 hour (or up to overnight) until firm.

Preheat Oven and Prepare Baking Sheets: Preheat your oven to 350°F (175°C). Line baking sheets with parchment paper.

Roll Out Dough: On a lightly floured surface, roll out one disk of dough to about 1/8-inch thickness. Use a round cookie cutter (about 2 inches in diameter) to cut out cookies. Repeat with the second disk of dough.

Cut Out Centers: Use a smaller round cookie cutter or a Linzer cookie cutter set with a decorative shape (such as a heart or star) to cut out the centers of half of the cookies. These will be the top cookies.

Bake Cookies: Place the cookies on the prepared baking sheets and bake in the preheated oven for 8-10 minutes, or until the edges are lightly golden. Remove from the oven and let the cookies cool on the baking sheets for a few minutes before transferring them to wire racks to cool completely.

Assemble Cookies: Spread a small amount of raspberry jam on the bottom (whole) cookies. Place a cut-out cookie (top cookie) on top of each jam-coated bottom cookie. Lightly press down to sandwich them together.

Dust with Powdered Sugar: Dust the tops of the assembled cookies with powdered sugar using a fine-mesh sieve.

Serve and Enjoy: These Hazelnut Linzer Cookies are elegant and delicious, perfect for holiday gatherings or special occasions!

These Hazelnut Linzer Cookies are a delightful twist on the classic Linzer cookies, featuring a rich hazelnut flavor and raspberry jam filling. Enjoy baking and sharing these beautiful and delicious cookies with family and friends!

M&M Christmas Cookies

Ingredients:

- 1 cup unsalted butter, softened
- 1 cup granulated sugar
- 1 cup light brown sugar, packed
- 2 large eggs
- 1 teaspoon vanilla extract
- 3 cups all-purpose flour
- 1 teaspoon baking soda
- 1/2 teaspoon salt
- 1 1/2 cups M&M's (holiday colors for festive cookies!)

Instructions:

Preheat Oven: Preheat your oven to 350°F (175°C). Line baking sheets with parchment paper or silicone mats.

Cream Butter and Sugars: In a large mixing bowl, cream together the softened butter, granulated sugar, and brown sugar until light and fluffy.

Add Eggs and Vanilla: Beat in the eggs, one at a time, until well combined. Add the vanilla extract and mix until incorporated.

Combine Dry Ingredients: In a separate bowl, whisk together the flour, baking soda, and salt.

Mix Wet and Dry Ingredients: Gradually add the dry ingredient mixture to the wet ingredients, mixing until just combined.

Add M&M's: Gently fold in the M&M's until evenly distributed in the cookie dough.

Drop Dough onto Baking Sheets: Drop rounded tablespoonfuls of dough onto the prepared baking sheets, spacing them about 2 inches apart.

Press Additional M&M's (Optional): If desired, press a few extra M&M's onto the tops of the dough balls for a more colorful appearance.

Bake: Bake in the preheated oven for 10-12 minutes or until the edges are golden brown and the centers are set.

Cool and Serve: Allow the cookies to cool on the baking sheets for a few minutes before transferring them to wire racks to cool completely.

Enjoy: These M&M Christmas Cookies are festive, chewy, and packed with colorful M&M's. They are perfect for holiday parties, cookie exchanges, or as a sweet treat for Santa!

Feel free to customize these cookies by using different colors of M&M's based on the occasion or holiday. Enjoy baking and sharing these delightful M&M Christmas Cookies with friends and family!

Snowball Cookies (Russian Tea Cakes)

Ingredients:

- 1 cup unsalted butter, softened
- 1/2 cup powdered sugar, plus more for coating
- 1 teaspoon vanilla extract
- 2 1/4 cups all-purpose flour
- 1/4 teaspoon salt
- 3/4 cup finely chopped pecans or walnuts

Instructions:

Preheat Oven: Preheat your oven to 375°F (190°C). Line baking sheets with parchment paper or silicone mats.

Cream Butter and Sugar: In a large mixing bowl, cream together the softened butter and powdered sugar until light and fluffy.

Add Vanilla and Flour: Mix in the vanilla extract. Gradually add the flour and salt, mixing until just combined.

Stir in Chopped Nuts: Fold in the finely chopped pecans or walnuts until evenly distributed in the dough.

Shape Dough into Balls: Roll tablespoon-sized portions of dough into balls and place them on the prepared baking sheets, spacing them about 1 inch apart.

Bake: Bake in the preheated oven for 10-12 minutes or until the bottoms of the cookies are lightly golden.

Cool Slightly: Allow the cookies to cool on the baking sheets for a few minutes.

Coat with Powdered Sugar: While the cookies are still warm, gently roll them in powdered sugar to coat completely.

Cool Completely and Re-Coat (Optional): Once the cookies are completely cooled, roll them again in powdered sugar for a thicker coating.

Serve and Enjoy: These Snowball Cookies, also known as Russian Tea Cakes, are buttery, nutty, and melt-in-your-mouth delicious! They are perfect for holiday gatherings or as a sweet treat with coffee or tea.

These classic Snowball Cookies are a favorite during the holiday season and are loved for their delicate texture and irresistible flavor. Enjoy making and savoring these delightful Snowball Cookies with your loved ones!

Candy Cane Cookies

Ingredients:

- 1 cup unsalted butter, softened
- 1 cup granulated sugar
- 1 teaspoon vanilla extract
- 1 teaspoon peppermint extract
- 1 large egg
- 3 cups all-purpose flour
- 1/2 teaspoon salt
- Red food coloring
- Crushed candy canes or peppermint candies, for garnish

Instructions:

Preheat Oven: Preheat your oven to 375°F (190°C). Line baking sheets with parchment paper or silicone mats.
Cream Butter and Sugar: In a large mixing bowl, cream together the softened butter and granulated sugar until light and fluffy.
Add Extracts and Egg: Mix in the vanilla extract, peppermint extract, and egg until well combined.
Combine Flour and Salt: In a separate bowl, whisk together the flour and salt.
Mix Wet and Dry Ingredients: Gradually add the flour mixture to the wet ingredients, mixing until a dough forms.
Divide Dough and Color: Divide the dough in half. Leave one half plain and add red food coloring to the other half, mixing until the color is evenly distributed.
Shape Candy Cane Cookies:
- Take a small portion of each dough (about 1 teaspoon each for small cookies) and roll them into ropes about 4 inches long.
- Place a red rope and a white rope side by side, press them together lightly, and twist to form a candy cane shape. Place the cookies on the prepared baking sheets, spacing them apart.

Bake: Bake in the preheated oven for 8-10 minutes or until the cookies are set and just beginning to turn golden around the edges.
Cool and Garnish: Remove the cookies from the oven and immediately sprinkle the tops with crushed candy canes or peppermint candies while they are still warm.

Cool Completely: Allow the cookies to cool on the baking sheets for a few minutes, then transfer them to wire racks to cool completely.
Serve and Enjoy: These festive Candy Cane Cookies are perfect for holiday parties, cookie exchanges, or as a sweet treat during the Christmas season!

These Candy Cane Cookies are not only delicious but also fun to make and share with family and friends. Enjoy baking and savoring these delightful and festive cookies!

Amaretti Cookies

Ingredients:

- 2 cups almond flour (finely ground almonds)
- 1 cup granulated sugar
- 2 large egg whites
- 1 teaspoon almond extract
- Powdered sugar, for dusting (optional)

Instructions:

Preheat Oven: Preheat your oven to 300°F (150°C). Line baking sheets with parchment paper.
Mix Almond Flour and Sugar: In a large bowl, combine the almond flour and granulated sugar.
Add Egg Whites and Almond Extract: In a separate bowl, whisk the egg whites until frothy. Add the almond extract to the egg whites and mix well.
Combine Wet and Dry Ingredients: Pour the egg white mixture into the almond flour mixture. Stir until a sticky dough forms.
Shape Dough into Balls: Take tablespoon-sized portions of dough and roll them into balls. Place the balls on the prepared baking sheets, spacing them about 2 inches apart.
Flatten Dough Balls (Optional): Use the back of a spoon or your fingertips to gently flatten each dough ball slightly.
Bake: Bake in the preheated oven for 20-25 minutes or until the cookies are set and lightly golden on the edges.
Cool and Dust with Powdered Sugar: Allow the cookies to cool on the baking sheets for a few minutes, then transfer them to wire racks to cool completely. Dust the cooled cookies with powdered sugar if desired.
Serve and Enjoy: These Amaretti Cookies are chewy, nutty, and delightful with a hint of almond flavor. They are perfect for serving with coffee or tea!

These traditional Italian Amaretti Cookies are gluten-free and easy to make with just a few simple ingredients. Enjoy baking and savoring these delicious Amaretti Cookies as a sweet treat for any occasion!

Apricot Kolaches

Ingredients:

- 1 cup unsalted butter, softened
- 8 oz cream cheese, softened
- 2 cups all-purpose flour
- 1/2 cup apricot preserves (or filling of your choice)
- Powdered sugar, for dusting

Instructions:

Prepare Dough: In a large mixing bowl, cream together the softened butter and cream cheese until smooth and well combined.

Add Flour: Gradually add the all-purpose flour to the creamed mixture, mixing until a soft dough forms. You can use a stand mixer fitted with a paddle attachment or mix by hand.

Chill Dough: Shape the dough into a ball, wrap it in plastic wrap, and refrigerate for at least 1 hour (or up to overnight) until firm.

Preheat Oven: Preheat your oven to 350°F (175°C). Line baking sheets with parchment paper or silicone mats.

Shape Kolaches: Roll out the chilled dough on a lightly floured surface to about 1/4-inch thickness. Use a round cookie cutter (about 2 inches in diameter) to cut out circles of dough.

Fill and Fold: Place a small spoonful of apricot preserves (or your desired filling) in the center of each dough circle. Fold the edges of the dough up and over the filling, pinching the seams together to seal and form a little pouch.

Bake: Place the filled kolaches on the prepared baking sheets, spacing them about 1 inch apart. Bake in the preheated oven for 12-15 minutes or until the edges are lightly golden.

Cool and Dust with Powdered Sugar: Allow the kolaches to cool on the baking sheets for a few minutes, then transfer them to wire racks to cool completely. Dust the cooled kolaches with powdered sugar before serving.

Serve and Enjoy: These Apricot Kolaches are soft, buttery pastries with a sweet apricot filling. They are perfect for breakfast, brunch, or as a delightful dessert!

These Apricot Kolaches are a wonderful treat to enjoy with a cup of coffee or tea. You can also experiment with different fillings such as raspberry, cherry, or poppy seed. Enjoy making and savoring these delicious homemade kolaches!

Fig Newtons

Ingredients:

- For the Fig Filling:
    - 2 cups dried figs, stems removed and chopped
    - 1/2 cup water
    - 1/4 cup honey or maple syrup
    - Zest of 1 lemon
    - Juice of 1 lemon
- For the Cookie Dough:
    - 1 cup unsalted butter, softened
    - 1 cup granulated sugar
    - 2 large eggs
    - 1 teaspoon vanilla extract
    - 2 1/2 cups all-purpose flour
    - 1/2 teaspoon baking powder
    - 1/2 teaspoon salt

Instructions:

Make the Fig Filling:
- In a medium saucepan, combine the chopped dried figs, water, honey or maple syrup, lemon zest, and lemon juice.
- Bring the mixture to a simmer over medium heat, then reduce the heat to low and cook for about 10-15 minutes, stirring occasionally, until the figs are soft and the mixture is thickened.
- Remove from heat and let the fig filling cool slightly. Transfer the mixture to a food processor or blender and blend until smooth. Set aside to cool completely.

Prepare the Cookie Dough:
- In a large mixing bowl, cream together the softened butter and granulated sugar until light and fluffy.
- Add the eggs, one at a time, beating well after each addition. Stir in the vanilla extract.

Combine Dry Ingredients:
- In a separate bowl, whisk together the flour, baking powder, and salt.

Mix Wet and Dry Ingredients:

- Gradually add the dry ingredient mixture to the wet ingredients, mixing until a soft dough forms.

Assemble the Fig Newtons:
- Preheat your oven to 350°F (175°C). Line a baking sheet with parchment paper.
- Divide the dough in half. Roll out one half of the dough on a lightly floured surface into a rectangle about 1/4-inch thick.
- Spread half of the cooled fig filling evenly over the dough rectangle.
- Roll the dough from one long side to enclose the filling, creating a log shape. Repeat with the remaining dough and filling.

Bake the Fig Newtons:
- Place the filled dough logs seam-side down on the prepared baking sheet.
- Bake in the preheated oven for 25-30 minutes or until the dough is lightly golden.
- Remove from the oven and let the logs cool on the baking sheet for about 10 minutes.

Slice and Serve:
- Transfer the cooled logs to a cutting board. Use a sharp knife to slice the logs into individual Fig Newtons, about 1-inch wide each.
- Store the Fig Newtons in an airtight container at room temperature. They can also be stored in the refrigerator for longer shelf life.

Enjoy Homemade Fig Newtons:
- These homemade Fig Newtons are soft, chewy, and filled with delicious fig flavor. Enjoy them as a nostalgic treat or a healthier alternative to store-bought versions!

This recipe yields wonderful homemade Fig Newtons that are perfect for snacking or enjoying with a cup of tea. Customize the filling with your favorite dried fruits for variety!

Cranberry Pistachio Shortbread

Ingredients:

- 1 cup (2 sticks) unsalted butter, softened
- 1/2 cup granulated sugar
- 2 cups all-purpose flour
- 1/4 teaspoon salt
- 1/2 cup dried cranberries, finely chopped
- 1/2 cup shelled pistachios, finely chopped
- Optional: Powdered sugar, for dusting

Instructions:

Preheat Oven: Preheat your oven to 350°F (175°C). Line a baking sheet with parchment paper or a silicone baking mat.

Cream Butter and Sugar: In a large mixing bowl, beat the softened butter and granulated sugar together until creamy and well combined.

Add Dry Ingredients: Gradually add the flour and salt to the butter-sugar mixture. Mix until the dough comes together and starts to form clumps.

Incorporate Cranberries and Pistachios: Fold in the chopped dried cranberries and chopped pistachios until evenly distributed throughout the dough.

Shape Dough:
- Divide the dough in half.
- Place each half of the dough onto a sheet of plastic wrap.
- Use the plastic wrap to help shape the dough into two logs, each about 1 1/2 inches in diameter. Roll them tightly in the plastic wrap.

Chill Dough: Refrigerate the wrapped dough logs for at least 1 hour, or until firm. For longer storage, you can freeze the dough for later use.

Slice Cookies:
- Once the dough is firm, unwrap the logs and use a sharp knife to slice them into rounds, about 1/4 to 1/2 inch thick.
- Place the slices on the prepared baking sheet, spacing them about 1 inch apart.

Bake: Bake in the preheated oven for 12-15 minutes, or until the edges of the cookies are lightly golden.

Cool and Dust (Optional):

- Allow the cookies to cool on the baking sheet for a few minutes, then transfer them to a wire rack to cool completely.
- If desired, dust the cooled cookies with powdered sugar before serving.

Serve and Enjoy:
- These Cranberry Pistachio Shortbread Cookies are buttery, rich, and perfect for any occasion.
- Enjoy them with a cup of tea or coffee, or package them as homemade gifts for friends and family during the holidays!

This recipe yields delightful Cranberry Pistachio Shortbread Cookies that are sure to impress with their festive colors and flavors. Enjoy baking and sharing these delicious treats!

Lemon Lavender Cookies

Ingredients:

- 1 cup unsalted butter, softened
- 1 cup granulated sugar
- Zest of 1 lemon
- 2 tablespoons fresh lemon juice
- 2 tablespoons dried culinary lavender (culinary grade, food-safe)
- 2 1/2 cups all-purpose flour
- 1/2 teaspoon baking powder
- 1/4 teaspoon salt
- Optional: Additional granulated sugar or powdered sugar for rolling

Instructions:

Preheat Oven: Preheat your oven to 350°F (175°C). Line baking sheets with parchment paper or silicone baking mats.

Cream Butter and Sugar: In a large mixing bowl, cream together the softened butter and granulated sugar until light and fluffy.

Add Lemon Zest, Juice, and Lavender: Mix in the lemon zest, lemon juice, and dried culinary lavender. Mix well to distribute the flavors.

Combine Dry Ingredients: In a separate bowl, whisk together the all-purpose flour, baking powder, and salt.

Mix Wet and Dry Ingredients: Gradually add the dry ingredient mixture to the wet ingredients, mixing until a soft dough forms.

Shape Dough into Balls (Optional):
- If desired, you can roll the dough into balls using about 1 tablespoon of dough for each cookie.
- Roll the balls in granulated sugar or powdered sugar for a sweet coating.

Flatten Dough (Alternative):
- Alternatively, you can refrigerate the dough for about 30 minutes to firm it up, then roll it out on a floured surface to about 1/4-inch thickness.
- Use cookie cutters to cut out shapes.

Bake Cookies:
- Place the shaped cookies on the prepared baking sheets, spacing them about 1 inch apart.

- Bake in the preheated oven for 10-12 minutes or until the edges are lightly golden.

Cool and Serve:
- Allow the cookies to cool on the baking sheets for a few minutes, then transfer them to wire racks to cool completely.

Enjoy:
- These Lemon Lavender Cookies are delicately flavored with a refreshing lemon taste and subtle floral notes from the lavender.
- Serve and enjoy these delightful cookies with tea or as a light dessert!

These Lemon Lavender Cookies are perfect for spring or summer gatherings, and they make a lovely treat for afternoon tea or special occasions. Enjoy baking and sharing these aromatic and flavorful cookies with your loved ones!

Maple Pecan Cookies

Ingredients:

- 1 cup unsalted butter, softened
- 1 cup packed light brown sugar
- 1/2 cup pure maple syrup
- 2 large eggs
- 1 teaspoon vanilla extract
- 3 cups all-purpose flour
- 1 teaspoon baking powder
- 1/2 teaspoon baking soda
- 1/2 teaspoon salt
- 1 cup chopped pecans

Instructions:

Preheat Oven: Preheat your oven to 350°F (175°C). Line baking sheets with parchment paper or silicone mats.

Cream Butter and Sugars: In a large mixing bowl, cream together the softened butter and brown sugar until light and fluffy.

Add Maple Syrup, Eggs, and Vanilla: Mix in the pure maple syrup, eggs, and vanilla extract until well combined.

Combine Dry Ingredients: In a separate bowl, whisk together the all-purpose flour, baking powder, baking soda, and salt.

Mix Wet and Dry Ingredients: Gradually add the dry ingredient mixture to the wet ingredients, mixing until just combined.

Fold in Chopped Pecans: Gently fold in the chopped pecans until evenly distributed in the cookie dough.

Drop Dough onto Baking Sheets: Drop rounded tablespoonfuls of dough onto the prepared baking sheets, spacing them about 2 inches apart.

Flatten Dough Balls (Optional): Use the back of a spoon or your fingertips to gently flatten each dough ball slightly.

Bake: Bake in the preheated oven for 10-12 minutes or until the edges are golden brown.

Cool and Serve: Allow the cookies to cool on the baking sheets for a few minutes before transferring them to wire racks to cool completely.

Enjoy: These Maple Pecan Cookies are chewy, flavorful, and perfect for maple syrup lovers! They are great for dessert or as a sweet snack.

Feel free to adjust the amount of maple syrup based on your preference for sweetness. These cookies will fill your kitchen with the wonderful aroma of maple and pecans as they bake. Enjoy making and savoring these delicious Maple Pecan Cookies!

Chocolate Hazelnut Biscotti

Ingredients:

- 1 3/4 cups all-purpose flour
- 1/2 cup unsweetened cocoa powder
- 1 teaspoon baking powder
- 1/4 teaspoon salt
- 1/2 cup unsalted butter, softened
- 1 cup granulated sugar
- 2 large eggs
- 1 teaspoon vanilla extract
- 1/2 cup chopped hazelnuts
- 1/2 cup semisweet chocolate chips or chunks

Instructions:

Preheat Oven and Prepare Baking Sheet: Preheat your oven to 350°F (175°C). Line a baking sheet with parchment paper or a silicone baking mat.

Mix Dry Ingredients: In a medium bowl, whisk together the all-purpose flour, cocoa powder, baking powder, and salt. Set aside.

Cream Butter and Sugar: In a large mixing bowl, cream together the softened butter and granulated sugar until light and fluffy.

Add Eggs and Vanilla: Beat in the eggs, one at a time, until well combined. Mix in the vanilla extract.

Incorporate Dry Ingredients: Gradually add the dry ingredient mixture to the wet ingredients, mixing until a dough forms.

Fold in Hazelnuts and Chocolate: Gently fold in the chopped hazelnuts and semisweet chocolate chips or chunks until evenly distributed in the dough.

Shape Dough into Logs: Divide the dough in half. On the prepared baking sheet, shape each half of the dough into a log about 12 inches long and 2 inches wide. Space the logs apart to allow for spreading during baking.

Bake First Round: Bake in the preheated oven for 25-30 minutes, or until the logs are firm to the touch. Remove from the oven and let cool for about 10 minutes.

Slice Biscotti: Using a serrated knife, slice the logs diagonally into 1/2-inch thick slices. Arrange the slices cut-side down on the baking sheet.

Bake Second Round: Bake the biscotti slices for an additional 10-12 minutes, flipping them halfway through, until they are crisp and dry.

Cool and Serve: Allow the biscotti to cool completely on wire racks. Once cooled, store them in an airtight container at room temperature.

Enjoy: These Chocolate Hazelnut Biscotti are perfect for dipping into coffee, tea, or hot chocolate. They also make lovely gifts or treats for gatherings!

These biscotti have a rich chocolate flavor complemented by crunchy hazelnuts and melty chocolate pieces. Enjoy making and savoring these delicious Chocolate Hazelnut Biscotti!

Orange Cardamom Cookies

Ingredients:

- 1 cup unsalted butter, softened
- 1 cup granulated sugar
- Zest of 1 large orange
- 2 large eggs
- 1 teaspoon vanilla extract
- 3 cups all-purpose flour
- 1 teaspoon baking powder
- 1/2 teaspoon salt
- 2 teaspoons ground cardamom
- Optional: Powdered sugar, for dusting

Instructions:

Preheat Oven: Preheat your oven to 350°F (175°C). Line baking sheets with parchment paper or silicone mats.

Cream Butter and Sugar: In a large mixing bowl, cream together the softened butter and granulated sugar until light and fluffy.

Add Orange Zest, Eggs, and Vanilla: Mix in the orange zest, eggs, and vanilla extract until well combined.

Combine Dry Ingredients: In a separate bowl, whisk together the all-purpose flour, baking powder, salt, and ground cardamom.

Mix Wet and Dry Ingredients: Gradually add the dry ingredient mixture to the wet ingredients, mixing until a dough forms.

Shape Dough into Balls (Optional):
- If desired, you can roll the dough into balls using about 1 tablespoon of dough for each cookie.
- Place the dough balls on the prepared baking sheets, spacing them about 2 inches apart.

Flatten Dough Balls (Optional): Use the back of a spoon or your fingertips to gently flatten each dough ball slightly.

Bake Cookies: Bake in the preheated oven for 10-12 minutes or until the edges are lightly golden.

Cool and Dust (Optional):
- Allow the cookies to cool on the baking sheets for a few minutes, then transfer them to wire racks to cool completely.

- If desired, dust the cooled cookies with powdered sugar before serving.

Enjoy: These Orange Cardamom Cookies are fragrant, flavorful, and perfect for citrus and spice lovers! They are great for dessert or as a sweet snack.

These cookies pair the bright, zesty flavor of orange with the warm, aromatic spice of cardamom for a delightful treat. Enjoy making and savoring these Orange Cardamom Cookies with your family and friends!

Brown Butter Snickerdoodles

Ingredients:

- 1 cup unsalted butter
- 1 cup granulated sugar
- 1/2 cup packed light brown sugar
- 2 large eggs
- 2 teaspoons vanilla extract
- 2 3/4 cups all-purpose flour
- 2 teaspoons cream of tartar
- 1 teaspoon baking soda
- 1/2 teaspoon salt

For Rolling:

- 1/4 cup granulated sugar
- 2 teaspoons ground cinnamon

Instructions:

Brown the Butter:
- In a saucepan, melt the butter over medium heat. Once melted, continue cooking, swirling the pan occasionally, until the butter turns a golden brown color and has a nutty aroma, about 3-5 minutes. Be careful not to burn the butter. Remove from heat and let it cool slightly.

Preheat Oven: Preheat your oven to 350°F (175°C). Line baking sheets with parchment paper or silicone mats.

Mix Sugars and Eggs: In a large mixing bowl, combine the granulated sugar, brown sugar, and slightly cooled brown butter. Mix until smooth and well combined.

Add Eggs and Vanilla: Beat in the eggs, one at a time, until incorporated. Stir in the vanilla extract.

Combine Dry Ingredients: In a separate bowl, whisk together the flour, cream of tartar, baking soda, and salt.

Mix Wet and Dry Ingredients: Gradually add the dry ingredient mixture to the wet ingredients, mixing until just combined.

Chill Dough (Optional): For easier handling, you can chill the dough in the refrigerator for about 30 minutes to 1 hour.

Make Cinnamon Sugar Mixture: In a small bowl, combine the granulated sugar and ground cinnamon for rolling.

Form Dough Balls: Roll tablespoon-sized portions of dough into balls, then roll each ball in the cinnamon sugar mixture to coat evenly.

Place on Baking Sheets: Arrange the coated dough balls on the prepared baking sheets, spacing them about 2 inches apart.

Bake: Bake in the preheated oven for 10-12 minutes, or until the edges are set and lightly golden.

Cool and Serve: Allow the cookies to cool on the baking sheets for a few minutes before transferring them to wire racks to cool completely.

Enjoy: These Brown Butter Snickerdoodles are wonderfully flavorful with a rich, nutty undertone from the brown butter. They are perfect for any occasion!

These cookies are a delightful twist on classic snickerdoodles, thanks to the addition of brown butter. Enjoy making and savoring these Brown Butter Snickerdoodles with friends and family!

Raspberry Almond Thumbprint Cookies

Ingredients:

- 1 cup unsalted butter, softened
- 2/3 cup granulated sugar
- 1/2 teaspoon almond extract
- 2 cups all-purpose flour
- 1/2 cup seedless raspberry jam
- Optional: Sliced almonds for garnish

Instructions:

Preheat Oven: Preheat your oven to 350°F (175°C). Line baking sheets with parchment paper or silicone mats.
Cream Butter and Sugar: In a large mixing bowl, cream together the softened butter and granulated sugar until light and fluffy.
Add Almond Extract and Flour: Mix in the almond extract. Gradually add the all-purpose flour, mixing until a dough forms.
Shape Dough into Balls: Roll tablespoon-sized portions of dough into balls and place them on the prepared baking sheets, spacing them about 1 inch apart.
Make Thumbprints: Use your thumb or the back of a small spoon to make an indentation in the center of each cookie.
Fill with Raspberry Jam: Spoon about 1/2 teaspoon of seedless raspberry jam into each indentation in the cookies.
Garnish (Optional): If desired, gently press a few sliced almonds around the edges of the jam-filled indentations.
Bake: Bake in the preheated oven for 10-12 minutes or until the edges are lightly golden.
Cool and Serve: Allow the cookies to cool on the baking sheets for a few minutes before transferring them to wire racks to cool completely.
Enjoy: These Raspberry Almond Thumbprint Cookies are delightful with a sweet and tangy raspberry filling and a buttery almond-flavored base.

These cookies are perfect for holiday gatherings, cookie exchanges, or any time you want a delicious treat with a burst of fruity flavor. Enjoy making and savoring these Raspberry Almond Thumbprint Cookies!

Chocolate Toffee Cookies

Ingredients:

- 1 cup unsalted butter, softened
- 1 cup granulated sugar
- 1 cup light brown sugar, packed
- 2 large eggs
- 1 teaspoon vanilla extract
- 2 cups all-purpose flour
- 3/4 cup unsweetened cocoa powder
- 1 teaspoon baking soda
- 1/2 teaspoon salt
- 1 cup toffee bits or chopped toffee pieces
- 1 cup semisweet chocolate chips

Instructions:

Preheat Oven: Preheat your oven to 350°F (175°C). Line baking sheets with parchment paper or silicone mats.

Cream Butter and Sugars: In a large mixing bowl, cream together the softened butter, granulated sugar, and brown sugar until light and fluffy.

Add Eggs and Vanilla: Beat in the eggs, one at a time, until well combined. Mix in the vanilla extract.

Combine Dry Ingredients: In a separate bowl, whisk together the all-purpose flour, cocoa powder, baking soda, and salt.

Mix Wet and Dry Ingredients: Gradually add the dry ingredient mixture to the wet ingredients, mixing until just combined.

Fold in Toffee and Chocolate Chips: Gently fold in the toffee bits or chopped toffee pieces and semisweet chocolate chips until evenly distributed in the cookie dough.

Drop Dough onto Baking Sheets: Drop rounded tablespoonfuls of dough onto the prepared baking sheets, spacing them about 2 inches apart.

Bake Cookies: Bake in the preheated oven for 10-12 minutes, or until the cookies are set and slightly firm around the edges.

Cool and Serve: Allow the cookies to cool on the baking sheets for a few minutes before transferring them to wire racks to cool completely.

Enjoy: These Chocolate Toffee Cookies are rich, chewy, and loaded with delicious chocolate and toffee flavors!

These cookies are perfect for chocolate and toffee lovers. They are great for parties, gatherings, or anytime you crave a decadent treat. Enjoy making and savoring these delightful Chocolate Toffee Cookies!

Molasses Crinkle Cookies

Ingredients:

- 3/4 cup unsalted butter, softened
- 1 cup granulated sugar
- 1/4 cup molasses
- 1 large egg
- 2 cups all-purpose flour
- 2 teaspoons baking soda
- 1/2 teaspoon salt
- 1 teaspoon ground cinnamon
- 1 teaspoon ground ginger
- 1/2 teaspoon ground cloves
- 1/2 cup granulated sugar (for rolling)

Instructions:

Preheat Oven: Preheat your oven to 375°F (190°C). Line baking sheets with parchment paper or silicone mats.
Cream Butter and Sugar: In a large mixing bowl, cream together the softened butter and 1 cup granulated sugar until light and fluffy.
Add Molasses and Egg: Mix in the molasses and egg until well combined.
Combine Dry Ingredients: In a separate bowl, whisk together the all-purpose flour, baking soda, salt, cinnamon, ginger, and cloves.
Mix Wet and Dry Ingredients: Gradually add the dry ingredient mixture to the wet ingredients, mixing until a soft dough forms.
Chill Dough (Optional): For easier handling, you can chill the dough in the refrigerator for about 30 minutes.
Roll Dough into Balls: Roll tablespoon-sized portions of dough into balls.
Roll in Sugar: Roll each dough ball in the remaining 1/2 cup granulated sugar until coated.
Place on Baking Sheets: Place the coated dough balls on the prepared baking sheets, spacing them about 2 inches apart.
Bake: Bake in the preheated oven for 8-10 minutes, or until the cookies are set and crackled on top.
Cool and Serve: Allow the cookies to cool on the baking sheets for a few minutes before transferring them to wire racks to cool completely.

Enjoy: These Molasses Crinkle Cookies are chewy, spiced, and perfect for the holiday season or any time of year!

These cookies have a wonderful blend of spices and the rich flavor of molasses. They are great for sharing with family and friends. Enjoy making and savoring these delicious Molasses Crinkle Cookies!

Matcha White Chocolate Cookies

Ingredients:

- 1 cup unsalted butter, softened
- 1 cup granulated sugar
- 2 large eggs
- 1 teaspoon vanilla extract
- 2 tablespoons matcha green tea powder
- 2 1/2 cups all-purpose flour
- 1 teaspoon baking powder
- 1/2 teaspoon salt
- 1 cup white chocolate chips or chunks

Instructions:

Preheat Oven: Preheat your oven to 350°F (175°C). Line baking sheets with parchment paper or silicone mats.
Cream Butter and Sugar: In a large mixing bowl, cream together the softened butter and granulated sugar until light and fluffy.
Add Eggs and Vanilla: Beat in the eggs, one at a time, until well combined. Mix in the vanilla extract.
Mix in Matcha Powder: Gradually add the matcha green tea powder to the butter mixture, mixing until evenly distributed and the dough turns green.
Combine Dry Ingredients: In a separate bowl, whisk together the all-purpose flour, baking powder, and salt.
Mix Wet and Dry Ingredients: Gradually add the dry ingredient mixture to the wet ingredients, mixing until just combined.
Fold in White Chocolate: Gently fold in the white chocolate chips or chunks until evenly distributed in the cookie dough.
Drop Dough onto Baking Sheets: Drop rounded tablespoonfuls of dough onto the prepared baking sheets, spacing them about 2 inches apart.
Flatten Dough (Optional): Use the back of a spoon or your fingertips to gently flatten each dough ball slightly.
Bake Cookies: Bake in the preheated oven for 10-12 minutes or until the edges are lightly golden.
Cool and Serve: Allow the cookies to cool on the baking sheets for a few minutes before transferring them to wire racks to cool completely.

Enjoy: These Matcha White Chocolate Cookies are uniquely flavored with a hint of green tea and studded with creamy white chocolate. They are perfect for tea time or as a special treat!

These cookies offer a delightful combination of earthy matcha and sweet white chocolate. Enjoy making and savoring these Matcha White Chocolate Cookies with a cup of hot tea or coffee!

Peanut Butter Blossoms

Ingredients:

- 1/2 cup unsalted butter, softened
- 1/2 cup creamy peanut butter
- 1/2 cup granulated sugar
- 1/2 cup packed light brown sugar
- 1 large egg
- 1 teaspoon vanilla extract
- 1 3/4 cups all-purpose flour
- 1 teaspoon baking soda
- 1/2 teaspoon salt
- Additional granulated sugar (for rolling)
- About 36 chocolate Hershey's Kisses, unwrapped

Instructions:

Preheat Oven: Preheat your oven to 375°F (190°C). Line baking sheets with parchment paper or silicone mats.
Cream Butter, Peanut Butter, and Sugars: In a large mixing bowl, cream together the softened butter, creamy peanut butter, granulated sugar, and brown sugar until smooth and creamy.
Add Egg and Vanilla: Beat in the egg and vanilla extract until well combined.
Combine Dry Ingredients: In a separate bowl, whisk together the all-purpose flour, baking soda, and salt.
Mix Wet and Dry Ingredients: Gradually add the dry ingredient mixture to the wet ingredients, mixing until just combined and a dough forms.
Shape Dough into Balls: Roll tablespoon-sized portions of dough into balls.
Roll in Sugar: Roll each dough ball in additional granulated sugar to coat.
Place on Baking Sheets: Place the coated dough balls on the prepared baking sheets, spacing them about 2 inches apart.
Bake: Bake in the preheated oven for 8-10 minutes, or until the edges are lightly golden.
Prepare Kisses: While the cookies are baking, unwrap the Hershey's Kisses.
Add Hershey's Kisses: As soon as the cookies come out of the oven, gently press a Hershey's Kiss into the center of each cookie.

Cool and Serve: Allow the cookies to cool on the baking sheets for a few minutes before transferring them to wire racks to cool completely.

Enjoy: These Peanut Butter Blossoms are classic and delicious, with a peanut butter cookie base and a chocolate center!

These cookies are a favorite during the holiday season and are perfect for any occasion.

Enjoy making and sharing these delightful Peanut Butter Blossoms with family and friends!

Chocolate Dipped Coconut Macaroons

Ingredients:

- 3 cups sweetened shredded coconut
- 3/4 cup sweetened condensed milk
- 1 teaspoon vanilla extract
- 1/4 teaspoon salt
- 2 large egg whites
- 4 ounces semi-sweet or dark chocolate, chopped
- 1 tablespoon coconut oil (optional, for smoother chocolate)

Instructions:

Preheat Oven: Preheat your oven to 325°F (160°C). Line a baking sheet with parchment paper.

Mix Coconut Mixture: In a large bowl, combine the sweetened shredded coconut, sweetened condensed milk, vanilla extract, and salt. Mix until well combined.

Whip Egg Whites: In a separate bowl, beat the egg whites until stiff peaks form.

Fold in Egg Whites: Gently fold the beaten egg whites into the coconut mixture until evenly incorporated.

Shape Macaroons: Use a spoon or cookie scoop to drop rounded tablespoonfuls of the coconut mixture onto the prepared baking sheet, spacing them about 1 inch apart.

Bake: Bake in the preheated oven for 20-25 minutes, or until the macaroons are golden brown on the bottom and edges. Let them cool completely on the baking sheet.

Prepare Chocolate: In a microwave-safe bowl or double boiler, melt the chopped chocolate and coconut oil (if using) until smooth, stirring at 30-second intervals.

Dip Macaroons: Dip the bottoms of each cooled macaroon into the melted chocolate, allowing any excess chocolate to drip off. Place the dipped macaroons back onto the parchment paper-lined baking sheet.

Set Chocolate: Place the baking sheet with dipped macaroons in the refrigerator for about 15-20 minutes, or until the chocolate sets.

Serve and Enjoy: Once the chocolate has set, your Chocolate-Dipped Coconut Macaroons are ready to enjoy! Store any leftovers in an airtight container at room temperature.

These Chocolate-Dipped Coconut Macaroons are a delightful combination of chewy coconut and rich chocolate. They make a wonderful treat for holidays, parties, or any time you crave a sweet indulgence! Enjoy making and savoring these delicious macaroons.

Cherry Chocolate Chip Cookies

Ingredients:

- 1 cup unsalted butter, softened
- 1 cup granulated sugar
- 1 cup packed light brown sugar
- 2 large eggs
- 1 teaspoon vanilla extract
- 3 cups all-purpose flour
- 1 teaspoon baking soda
- 1/2 teaspoon salt
- 1 cup semisweet chocolate chips
- 1 cup dried cherries (sweetened or unsweetened)

Instructions:

Preheat Oven: Preheat your oven to 375°F (190°C). Line baking sheets with parchment paper or silicone mats.
Cream Butter and Sugars: In a large mixing bowl, cream together the softened butter, granulated sugar, and brown sugar until light and fluffy.
Add Eggs and Vanilla: Beat in the eggs, one at a time, until well combined. Mix in the vanilla extract.
Combine Dry Ingredients: In a separate bowl, whisk together the all-purpose flour, baking soda, and salt.
Mix Wet and Dry Ingredients: Gradually add the dry ingredient mixture to the wet ingredients, mixing until just combined.
Fold in Chocolate Chips and Cherries: Gently fold in the semisweet chocolate chips and dried cherries until evenly distributed in the cookie dough.
Drop Dough onto Baking Sheets: Drop rounded tablespoonfuls of dough onto the prepared baking sheets, spacing them about 2 inches apart.
Bake Cookies: Bake in the preheated oven for 10-12 minutes or until the edges are golden brown.
Cool and Serve: Allow the cookies to cool on the baking sheets for a few minutes before transferring them to wire racks to cool completely.
Enjoy: These Cherry Chocolate Chip Cookies are a delightful combination of sweet and tart flavors with bursts of chocolate. They are perfect for any occasion!

These cookies are great for holiday baking, potlucks, or simply as a special treat. Enjoy making and savoring these Cherry Chocolate Chip Cookies with your loved ones!

Oatmeal Raisin Cookies

Ingredients:

- 1 cup unsalted butter, softened
- 1 cup packed light brown sugar
- 1/2 cup granulated sugar
- 2 large eggs
- 1 teaspoon vanilla extract
- 1 1/2 cups all-purpose flour
- 1 teaspoon baking soda
- 1 teaspoon ground cinnamon
- 1/2 teaspoon salt
- 3 cups old-fashioned rolled oats
- 1 cup raisins (or more, as desired)

Instructions:

Preheat Oven: Preheat your oven to 350°F (175°C). Line baking sheets with parchment paper or silicone mats.
Cream Butter and Sugars: In a large mixing bowl, cream together the softened butter, brown sugar, and granulated sugar until light and fluffy.
Add Eggs and Vanilla: Beat in the eggs, one at a time, until well combined. Mix in the vanilla extract.
Combine Dry Ingredients: In a separate bowl, whisk together the all-purpose flour, baking soda, ground cinnamon, and salt.
Mix Wet and Dry Ingredients: Gradually add the dry ingredient mixture to the wet ingredients, mixing until just combined.
Fold in Oats and Raisins: Gently fold in the rolled oats and raisins until evenly distributed in the cookie dough.
Drop Dough onto Baking Sheets: Drop rounded tablespoonfuls of dough onto the prepared baking sheets, spacing them about 2 inches apart.
Flatten Dough (Optional): Use the back of a spoon or your fingertips to gently flatten each dough ball slightly.
Bake Cookies: Bake in the preheated oven for 10-12 minutes, or until the edges are golden brown.
Cool and Serve: Allow the cookies to cool on the baking sheets for a few minutes before transferring them to wire racks to cool completely.

Enjoy: These classic Oatmeal Raisin Cookies are chewy, hearty, and packed with delicious flavors. They are perfect for sharing with friends and family!

Feel free to adjust the amount of raisins or add chopped nuts if desired. These cookies are a comforting treat that pairs well with a glass of milk or a cup of tea. Enjoy making and savoring these Oatmeal Raisin Cookies!

Brownie Cookies

Ingredients:

- 1/2 cup unsalted butter
- 8 ounces semisweet or bittersweet chocolate, chopped
- 1 cup granulated sugar
- 3 large eggs
- 1 teaspoon vanilla extract
- 1 cup all-purpose flour
- 2 tablespoons unsweetened cocoa powder
- 1/4 teaspoon salt
- 1/2 teaspoon baking powder
- 1 cup semisweet chocolate chips (optional)

Instructions:

Preheat Oven: Preheat your oven to 350°F (175°C). Line baking sheets with parchment paper or silicone mats.

Melt Butter and Chocolate: In a microwave-safe bowl or over a double boiler, melt the butter and chopped chocolate until smooth. Stir until well combined and set aside to cool slightly.

Mix Sugar, Eggs, and Vanilla: In a large mixing bowl, whisk together the granulated sugar, eggs, and vanilla extract until smooth.

Add Melted Chocolate Mixture: Gradually add the melted chocolate mixture to the sugar and egg mixture, stirring until well combined.

Combine Dry Ingredients: In a separate bowl, whisk together the all-purpose flour, unsweetened cocoa powder, salt, and baking powder.

Mix Wet and Dry Ingredients: Gradually add the dry ingredient mixture to the wet ingredients, mixing until just combined.

Fold in Chocolate Chips (Optional): Gently fold in the semisweet chocolate chips until evenly distributed in the cookie dough.

Chill Dough (Optional): For easier handling, you can chill the dough in the refrigerator for about 30 minutes.

Drop Dough onto Baking Sheets: Drop rounded tablespoonfuls of dough onto the prepared baking sheets, spacing them about 2 inches apart.

Bake Cookies: Bake in the preheated oven for 10-12 minutes, or until the edges are set and the tops have cracked slightly.

Cool and Serve: Allow the cookies to cool on the baking sheets for a few minutes before transferring them to wire racks to cool completely.
Enjoy: These Brownie Cookies are rich, fudgy, and perfect for chocolate lovers! They have a brownie-like texture with a crispy exterior.

These cookies are delicious on their own or served with a scoop of ice cream for a decadent dessert. Enjoy making and savoring these delightful Brownie Cookies!

Espresso Chocolate Shortbread

Ingredients:

- 1 cup unsalted butter, softened
- 1/2 cup granulated sugar
- 2 teaspoons instant espresso powder or instant coffee granules
- 2 cups all-purpose flour
- 1/4 cup unsweetened cocoa powder
- 1/4 teaspoon salt
- 1/2 cup semisweet or dark chocolate chips or chunks

For Espresso Glaze (Optional):

- 1 teaspoon instant espresso powder or instant coffee granules
- 1 tablespoon hot water
- 1 cup powdered sugar
- 1-2 tablespoons milk or cream

Instructions:

Preheat Oven: Preheat your oven to 350°F (175°C). Line baking sheets with parchment paper or silicone mats.

Cream Butter, Sugar, and Espresso: In a large mixing bowl, cream together the softened butter, granulated sugar, and instant espresso powder until light and fluffy.

Add Dry Ingredients: Gradually add the all-purpose flour, unsweetened cocoa powder, and salt to the butter mixture. Mix until a dough forms.

Fold in Chocolate Chips: Gently fold in the semisweet or dark chocolate chips or chunks until evenly distributed in the dough.

Shape Dough: Shape the dough into a disc and wrap it in plastic wrap. Chill in the refrigerator for at least 30 minutes.

Roll and Cut Cookies: On a lightly floured surface, roll out the chilled dough to about 1/4-inch thickness. Use cookie cutters to cut out desired shapes (such as circles or squares) or use a knife to cut into bars or wedges.

Bake Cookies: Place the cut cookies on the prepared baking sheets. Bake in the preheated oven for 12-15 minutes, or until the edges are set.

Cool Cookies: Allow the cookies to cool on the baking sheets for a few minutes before transferring them to wire racks to cool completely.

Prepare Espresso Glaze (Optional):
- In a small bowl, dissolve the instant espresso powder or coffee granules in hot water.
- Whisk in the powdered sugar until smooth and well combined.
- Gradually add milk or cream, 1 tablespoon at a time, until the glaze reaches your desired consistency.

Glaze Cookies (Optional): Once the cookies are completely cooled, drizzle or spread the espresso glaze over the cookies using a spoon or piping bag.

Allow Glaze to Set: Let the glaze set before serving or storing the cookies.

Enjoy: These Espresso Chocolate Shortbread Cookies are rich, buttery, and infused with a delightful coffee flavor. They are perfect with a cup of coffee or tea!

These cookies are a sophisticated treat that combines the flavors of chocolate and espresso. Enjoy making and savoring these Espresso Chocolate Shortbread Cookies for a special occasion or anytime you want a delicious indulgence.

Lemon Poppy Seed Cookies

Ingredients:

- 1 cup unsalted butter, softened
- 1 cup granulated sugar
- Zest of 2 lemons
- 2 tablespoons fresh lemon juice
- 2 large eggs
- 1 teaspoon vanilla extract
- 3 cups all-purpose flour
- 1 tablespoon poppy seeds
- 1 teaspoon baking powder
- 1/2 teaspoon salt
- Optional: Powdered sugar for dusting

Instructions:

Preheat Oven: Preheat your oven to 350°F (175°C). Line baking sheets with parchment paper or silicone mats.
Cream Butter, Sugar, and Lemon Zest: In a large mixing bowl, cream together the softened butter, granulated sugar, and lemon zest until light and fluffy.
Add Lemon Juice, Eggs, and Vanilla: Mix in the fresh lemon juice, eggs, and vanilla extract until well combined.
Combine Dry Ingredients: In a separate bowl, whisk together the all-purpose flour, poppy seeds, baking powder, and salt.
Mix Wet and Dry Ingredients: Gradually add the dry ingredient mixture to the wet ingredients, mixing until just combined and a dough forms.
Shape Dough into Balls: Roll tablespoon-sized portions of dough into balls and place them on the prepared baking sheets, spacing them about 2 inches apart.
Flatten Dough Balls (Optional): Use the back of a spoon or your fingertips to gently flatten each dough ball slightly.
Bake Cookies: Bake in the preheated oven for 10-12 minutes, or until the edges are lightly golden.
Cool and Dust (Optional):
- Allow the cookies to cool on the baking sheets for a few minutes, then transfer them to wire racks to cool completely.
- If desired, dust the cooled cookies with powdered sugar before serving.

Enjoy: These Lemon Poppy Seed Cookies are bright, zesty, and perfect for citrus lovers! They are great for dessert or as a sweet snack.

These cookies offer a delightful combination of lemon flavor and crunchy poppy seeds. Enjoy making and savoring these Lemon Poppy Seed Cookies with a refreshing cup of tea or coffee!

Fig and Walnut Rugelach

Ingredients:

For the Rugelach Dough:

- 1 cup unsalted butter, softened
- 8 oz cream cheese, softened
- 2 cups all-purpose flour
- 1/4 teaspoon salt
- 1/4 cup granulated sugar
- 1 teaspoon vanilla extract

For the Filling:

- 1 cup dried figs, finely chopped
- 1 cup walnuts, finely chopped
- 1/2 cup brown sugar
- 1 teaspoon ground cinnamon
- 1/4 teaspoon ground nutmeg
- Zest of 1 orange
- 1/4 cup apricot preserves, warmed (for brushing)

For Dusting:

- Powdered sugar (optional)

Instructions:

Prepare the Rugelach Dough:
- In a large bowl, beat together the softened butter and cream cheese until smooth.
- Add the flour, salt, granulated sugar, and vanilla extract. Mix until the dough comes together and forms a ball.
- Divide the dough into 4 equal portions, shape each portion into a disk, wrap in plastic wrap, and refrigerate for at least 1 hour (or up to overnight).

Make the Filling:

- In a medium bowl, combine the chopped dried figs, chopped walnuts, brown sugar, ground cinnamon, ground nutmeg, and orange zest. Mix well to combine.

Assemble the Rugelach:
- Preheat your oven to 350°F (175°C). Line baking sheets with parchment paper.
- Take one disk of dough out of the refrigerator and roll it out on a lightly floured surface into a 10-inch circle (about 1/8 inch thick).
- Spread a thin layer of apricot preserves over the dough circle.
- Sprinkle about 1/4 of the fig and walnut filling evenly over the dough.
- Using a pizza cutter or sharp knife, cut the dough into 12 equal wedges (like slicing a pizza).
- Starting from the wider end of each wedge, roll up the dough tightly to form a crescent shape.
- Place the rugelach, seam side down, on the prepared baking sheets, spacing them slightly apart.

Bake the Rugelach:
- Bake in the preheated oven for 20-25 minutes, or until golden brown.
- Remove from the oven and let the rugelach cool on the baking sheets for 5 minutes, then transfer to wire racks to cool completely.

Optional Dusting:
- Once cooled, dust the rugelach with powdered sugar for an extra touch of sweetness.

Enjoy: These Fig and Walnut Rugelach cookies are best enjoyed with a cup of tea or coffee. Store any leftovers in an airtight container at room temperature.

This recipe yields delicious, flaky rugelach filled with sweet figs, crunchy walnuts, and warm spices. They make a wonderful treat for holidays or any special occasion. Enjoy making and savoring these delightful Fig and Walnut Rugelach cookies!

Chocolate Cherry Blossoms

Ingredients:

- 1 cup all-purpose flour
- 1/3 cup unsweetened cocoa powder
- 1/4 teaspoon salt
- 1/2 cup unsalted butter, softened
- 2/3 cup granulated sugar
- 1 large egg yolk
- 2 tablespoons milk
- 1 teaspoon vanilla extract
- 1 cup semisweet chocolate chips or chunks
- 24 maraschino cherries, drained and patted dry
- Additional granulated sugar for rolling

Instructions:

Preheat Oven: Preheat your oven to 350°F (175°C). Line baking sheets with parchment paper or silicone mats.

Prepare Dry Ingredients: In a bowl, whisk together the flour, cocoa powder, and salt. Set aside.

Cream Butter and Sugar: In a separate large bowl, cream together the softened butter and granulated sugar until light and fluffy.

Add Egg Yolk, Milk, and Vanilla: Beat in the egg yolk, milk, and vanilla extract until well combined.

Mix Wet and Dry Ingredients: Gradually add the dry ingredient mixture to the wet ingredients, mixing until a dough forms.

Fold in Chocolate Chips: Gently fold in the semisweet chocolate chips or chunks until evenly distributed in the dough.

Shape Dough Balls: Roll tablespoon-sized portions of dough into balls.

Roll in Sugar: Roll each dough ball in granulated sugar to coat.

Place on Baking Sheets: Place the coated dough balls on the prepared baking sheets, spacing them about 2 inches apart.

Make Indentations and Add Cherries: Use your thumb or the back of a spoon to make an indentation in the center of each dough ball. Place a maraschino cherry into each indentation.

Bake Cookies: Bake in the preheated oven for 10-12 minutes, or until the edges are set.

Cool and Serve: Allow the cookies to cool on the baking sheets for a few minutes before transferring them to wire racks to cool completely.

Enjoy: These Chocolate Cherry Blossom Cookies are a delightful combination of rich chocolate and sweet cherry. They are perfect for holiday baking or any occasion!

These cookies are sure to be a hit with chocolate and cherry lovers. Enjoy making and savoring these Chocolate Cherry Blossom Cookies with their delightful flavors and festive appearance!

Chocolate Gingerbread Cookies

Ingredients:

- 2 cups all-purpose flour
- 1/4 cup unsweetened cocoa powder
- 1 teaspoon ground ginger
- 1 teaspoon ground cinnamon
- 1/2 teaspoon ground cloves
- 1/2 teaspoon baking soda
- 1/4 teaspoon salt
- 1/2 cup unsalted butter, softened
- 1/2 cup granulated sugar
- 1/2 cup molasses
- 1 large egg
- 1 teaspoon vanilla extract
- 1 cup semisweet or dark chocolate chips or chunks
- Optional: Powdered sugar for dusting

Instructions:

Preheat Oven: Preheat your oven to 350°F (175°C). Line baking sheets with parchment paper or silicone mats.

Combine Dry Ingredients: In a medium bowl, whisk together the flour, cocoa powder, ground ginger, ground cinnamon, ground cloves, baking soda, and salt. Set aside.

Cream Butter and Sugar: In a large bowl, cream together the softened butter and granulated sugar until light and fluffy.

Add Molasses, Egg, and Vanilla: Mix in the molasses, egg, and vanilla extract until well combined.

Mix Wet and Dry Ingredients: Gradually add the dry ingredient mixture to the wet ingredients, mixing until a dough forms.

Fold in Chocolate Chips: Gently fold in the semisweet or dark chocolate chips or chunks until evenly distributed in the dough.

Chill Dough (Optional): For easier handling, you can chill the dough in the refrigerator for about 30 minutes.

Shape Dough Balls: Roll tablespoon-sized portions of dough into balls and place them on the prepared baking sheets, spacing them about 2 inches apart.

Flatten Dough Balls (Optional): Use the back of a spoon or your fingertips to gently flatten each dough ball slightly.

Bake Cookies: Bake in the preheated oven for 10-12 minutes, or until the edges are set.

Cool and Dust (Optional):
- Allow the cookies to cool on the baking sheets for a few minutes, then transfer them to wire racks to cool completely.
- If desired, dust the cooled cookies with powdered sugar for decoration.

Enjoy: These Chocolate Gingerbread Cookies combine the warm spices of traditional gingerbread with rich chocolate flavor. They are perfect for holiday baking or anytime you crave a festive treat!

Feel free to adjust the spice levels according to your preference. These cookies are deliciously soft and chewy with a delightful chocolate twist. Enjoy making and savoring these Chocolate Gingerbread Cookies!

www.ingramcontent.com/pod-product-compliance
Lightning Source LLC
LaVergne TN
LVHW081606060526
838201LV00054B/2101